MOROCCO
MEDITERRANEAN CUISINE

MOROCCO
MEDITERRANEAN CUISINE

KÖNEMANN

Contents

List of Recipes

Level of difficulty:

★   Easy
★★   Medium
★★★   Difficult

Soups   38

Hot & Cold Appetizers   8

Tagines & Couscous   60

Fish & Seafood 92

Meat & Poultry 112

Desserts & Pastries 146

Hot & Cold
Appetizers

Briouates

Preparation time:	30 minutes
Cooking time:	10 minutes
Difficulty:	★★

Serves 4

Briouates:

14 oz/400 g	small shrimp, ready to cook
2 tbsp/30ml	olive oil
7 oz/200 g	yufka pastry dough sheets
1	egg
	oil for frying

For the chermoula sauce:

2 oz/50 g	fresh cilantro (coriander)
2 oz/50 g	flat-leaf parsley
1 oz/30 g	garlic
7 oz/200 g	onions
3½ oz/100 g	red olives
¼ tsp	ground cumin
½ tsp	paprika
7 tbsp/100 ml	olive oil
1	lemon
	salt and pepper

For the garnish:

3½ oz/100 g	strips of pickled lemon
1 tsp/5 g	paprika
3½ oz/100 g	harissa

The term *briouate* refers to stuffed envelopes of *yufka* (pastry made from unleavened dough and rolled into sheets), deep-fried golden-brown. They can be of different shapes: rectangular, triangular or round. Mohammed Aïtali has decided on a filling of shrimp and *chermoula* sauce, but there are many other tasty variations based on chicken, seafood, sweet rice, goat's cheese, or almond honey.

Little common shrimp are excellent for filling *briouates*. In Morocco, they are available all the year round although they are more difficult to find during winter, as the conditions for fishermen are more difficult then. These small shrimp live on the shores of the northern Atlantic in great numbers. The Moroccans eat them with enthusiasm, as they do the medium-sized gray-shelled scampi and intensely red deep-sea shrimp. Mixed with *chermoula*,

these crustaceans can also be made into a ragout, known locally as a tagine.

Chermoula, sometimes used as a marinade and sometimes as a sauce, is an essential element in Moroccan cuisine. This mixture of parsley, garlic, cumin, paprika and oil goes wonderfully with shrimp, but also with most fish dishes, whether the fish is fried, poached, baked, or used as an ingredient in a tagine. It also serves to flavor lentil or poultry dishes. *Chermoula* can be prepared in advance and kept in a tightly closed container in the fridge.

Red olives are at a particular stage of ripeness between green and black olives. As with green olives, they are often used to garnish or are cooked with the dish.

For the chermoula, mix cilantro, parsley, garlic, onions, chopped red olives, and ground cumin, salt, pepper, and paprika. Add 2 tsp of lemon juice and a dash of olive oil.

Place the washed shrimp in a bowl. Add chermoula sauce and mix well.

Heat olive oil in a frying pan and add the shrimp and chermoula mixture. Cook the mixture on a high heat, stirring continuously, until golden-brown.

with Shrimp

Layer and roll several layers of yufka pastry. Cut the roll into 3 or 4 equal-sized portions and then unroll to form strips of pastry. Separate the individual strips.

Beat the egg in a bowl. Place a little of the shrimp-chermoula mixture at the end of a strip of pastry and fold it from left to right and back again to form a triangle, until you are left with a triangular filled "envelope," the briouate. Stick down using the beaten egg.

Heat the oil in a saucepan or deep fryer. Dip the briouates into the oil using a wire basket or slotted spatula and fry till golden-brown. Take out and drain on paper towels. Place on a plate, garnish, and serve warm.

Jban Briouates

Preparation time: 30 minutes
Cooking time: 3–4 minutes
Difficulty: ★

Serves 4

3½ oz/100 g	black pitted olives
½ bunch	cilantro (coriander)
2 pieces	*jban* (fresh goat's cheese)
	white pepper

2	eggs
1¼ lbs/500 g	*yufka* pastry dough sheets
	oil for frying

For the garnish:

1	tomato
	leaves of mint

If you travel to the Fez region, you will certainly have the opportunity of tasting the famous *briouates*. In a menu of several courses, these dainty little bites are served as an appetizer or a dessert. Their fillings vary according to what the chef puts in them or what is available on the market. Some prepare them with chicken, pigeon, spinach, or shrimp. Others prefer almond paste or honey.

You can let your imagination run free when preparing the fillings. The chef for this dish has decided on *jban*, the typical Moroccan soft goat's cheese. This cheese is generally used in sweet cookies and cakes, and is made only from goat's milk. It contains less than 45 percent fat and has a sweetish, sometimes slightly sour aroma. If you cannot get hold of it, ricotta is also suitable, but it has a much more neutral taste.

In this recipe the cilantro gives the goat's cheese its special aroma. Cilantro—coriander leaf—is an important ingredient in many Arab dishes, from salads, soups, and ragouts to fish. Black olives are particularly favored in the Mediterranean, and are pickled in brine. Even if they are rinsed, they don't lose their salty taste. Remember this when seasoning!

In Morocco, cooking is unthinkable without sheets of *yufka* pastry. These are made from flour, salt, and water only, and in earlier years families made them themselves. Experience is necessary for their preparation. Wherever *yufka* pastry sheets are still made by hand, this is done by very experienced women who still use the *tabsil dial ouarqua*, a copper tray with a tin-plated surface on which the pastry sheets can be heated.

Dice the black olives into small pieces on the work surface.

Wash the cilantro and chop finely with a large knife.

In a bowl, mix the goat's cheese, diced olives, and chopped cilantro.

with Cilantro

Season with pepper. Break 1 egg into a small bowl, beat and add to the salad bowl. Mix using a wooden spoon.

Using a long knife, cut the yufka pastry lengthways into strips. Break the second egg into a small bowl, beat and put aside.

Place a little filling onto each strip. Then fold from left to right to make a closed triangle. Stick down the end with beaten egg. Deep-fry for 3–4 minutes. Drain. Arrange on serving platters and garnish with a piece of tomato and fresh mint.

M'hancha with

Preparation time: 50 minutes
Cooking time: 30 minutes
Difficulty: ★★★

Serves 4

7 oz/200 g each	carrots, turnips, potatoes, and peas
2¼ lbs/1 kg	spinach
2½ sticks/300 g	butter
1 tsp each	paprika and cumin
3 stems	flat-leaf parsley
3 stems	cilantro (coriander)
1 clove	garlic
10 sheets	*yufka* pastry dough
1	egg
	salt

For the filling:

1⅛ lbs/500 g	ground beef
7 oz/200 g	onions
3 cloves	garlic
½ bunch	parsley
½ bunch	cilantro (coriander)
2 leaves	fresh mint
1 stem	marjoram
½ tsp	ground ginger
½ tsp	ground paprika
1 tsp	ground cinnamon
½ tsp	cumin
2 tbsp/30 ml	vegetable oil
3	eggs
	salt and pepper

For the garnish:

	lemon
	tomatoes

In cooking, things are always changing, and *m'hancha* is a good example. This traditional almond-based pastry dish is an important part of Moroccan cuisine and is forever being adapted and refined. Savory versions of the originally sweet pastry dish with its snail shape (hence its name) are being devised these days.

This very light dish requires some skill. The challenge consists in getting the sheets of pastry into the right shape, on no account must they tear. You will need patience and skill for this dish!

This specialty is prepared using many vegetables and is rich in vitamins. Generally, Moroccans use wild mallow, a plant native to Morocco. We have replaced it with spinach, which is more readily available. Spinach originates in

Persia and is eaten raw in salads or cooked. The leaves should be well shaped, free of blemishes and undamaged. Before you blanch them, we recommend that you wash them under running water and don't leave them lying in water.

Peas are in season in spring and early summer and go well with mint, which can be put into the cooking water. Peas can easily be shelled by hand and need not be washed. The pods should be bright green and firm. They will keep in the fridge for two to three days, but should be used as fresh as possible.

Khadija Bensdira's *m'hancha* also makes a good main course. This original and delicious dish is really something for the gourmet.

Peel and finely dice carrots, turnips, and potatoes. Shell peas. Wash spinach. Blanch all vegetables separately in salted water.

Melt ½ stick/50 g butter in a pan. Add blanched spinach and sweat with paprika powder, chopped parsley and chopped cilantro, cumin, and crushed garlic clove. Put aside.

For the filling, brown the beef in oil. Add finely chopped onions, crushed garlic, chopped parsley, and chopped cilantro, torn mint, and marjoram. Season with ginger, paprika, cinnamon, and cumin. Add salt and pepper.

Spring Vegetables

Add 3 eggs to the mixture and stir.

Add blanched, diced carrots, turnips, and potatoes, peas, and spinach. Break the remaining egg and put the yolk in a bowl.

Spread out the sheets of pastry. Spread the filling across the whole width. Roll the sheets up to join together and shape into a spiral. Stick down the ends with the egg yolk. Spread the remaining butter over the m'hancha. Bake in an oven for 12 minutes at 350 °F/180 °C. Garnish and serve.

Seafood and

Preparation time: 1 hour
Soaking time: 15 minutes
Cooking time: 35 minutes
Difficulty: ★★★

Serves 4

3 oz/80 g	Chinese thread noodles
10 oz/300 g	button mushrooms
11 oz/320 g	chicken
3½ oz/100 g	calamaries (small squid)
1 tbsp/15 ml	olive oil
7 tbsp/100 ml	peanut oil
4	medium onions
2 cloves	garlic
1 tsp/5 g	saffron threads

½ envelope	Moroccan saffron for coloring
1 pinch	ginger
1½ tsp	paprika powder
2	fillets of white fish
3½ oz/100 g	small shrimp, boiled and shelled
1 bunch	fresh cilantro (coriander)
1 bunch	flat-leaf parsley
½ stick/60 g	fresh (unsalted) butter
1	lemon
1	egg yolk
8 sheets	*yufka* pastry dough
	salt and pepper

Traditionally, *m'hancha* are served as sweet pastries; the sheets of pastry are filled with a sweet almond mixture, rolled up and formed into a spiral shape. Between 1993 and 1994, Bouchaïb Kama developed a savory version for the Farah restaurant and hotel in Casablanca. This is filled with chicken, seafood, button mushrooms, and Chinese thread noodles. After being promoted on various TV programs, the recipe has motivated other chefs and restaurateurs to serve this dish at weddings and receptions.

The chef recommends using small shrimp for the filling. In the seas around Morocco, there are many varieties of shrimp, and all of them are delicious. Among the best known are the blue shrimp, the fat *bouark*, common shrimp, scampi, and various deep-sea shrimp with bright red shells.

Calamaries (small squid) require careful preparation. Cut off the head, draw out the intestines and the bone, then turn the mantle inside-out like a glove and rinse off any remaining sand.

Your choice of seafood will naturally depend on what is available in the market. It is then up to you whether to use shellfish, such as shrimp, mussels, cockles, scallops, or fillets of fish such as sea bass, shi drum, John Dory, or sole.

When frying the diced chicken together with the button mushrooms, you can add fish or shrimp stock to braise the ingredients and add flavor. Let the filling cool before rolling it up in the pastry sheets, to avoid the *m'hancha* splitting during baking.

Soak the noodles. Dice the mushrooms and chicken. Clean and gut the calamaries. Fry the chopped onions, garlic, and saffron threads, in 1 tbsp each of olive and peanut oil. Add the chicken, calamaries, button mushrooms, salt, pepper, saffron powder, ginger, and paprika.

Allow the ingredients to simmer for 8 minutes, then stir in the thread noodles, cut small with a knife. Cook for 6–8 minutes. Add fish fillets and shrimp. Cook for a further 8–10 minutes.

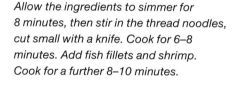

After cooking, add cilantro and parsley, both finely chopped. Stir once more.

Chicken M'hancha

Spoon in the butter to make the filling smooth. Squeeze the lemon over it and mix in the juice. Transfer the filling to a plate and allow to cool. Meanwhile, beat 1 egg yolk in a small bowl.

Spread 2 sheets of pastry out on the work surface. Place a strip of filling on one end of the sheets. Roll up carefully but firmly from top to bottom. Stick down the ends of the roll with the beaten egg yolk.

Spread peanut oil over the roll. Carefully shape it into a spiral (m'hancha). Coat the end, once again, with egg yolk. Form a further 3 spirals in the same way and then bake all of them in the oven on an oiled baking sheet for about 5 minutes at 400 °F/200 °C.

Pastelitos

Preparation time: 1 hour
Cooking time: 30 minutes
Difficulty: ★★

Serves 4

For the filling (miga):

1 1/8 lbs/500 g	ground beef
1	onion
1/2 bunch	parsley
2	bay leaves
1/2 tsp	mace
1/2 tsp	turmeric
1/2 tsp	ground nutmeg
	salt and pepper

For the pastelito dough:

3	eggs
3/4 cup/190 ml	vegetable oil
1 tsp	baking soda
4 cups/450 g	flour
4 tbsp	goose fat
	salt
	oil for frying

Pastelitos de ojas are very tasty filled envelopes of flaky pastry. This specialty of Tangier's Jewish community is usually prepared for festive occasions. Some families also prepare *pastelitos* with honey and almonds, which are served as dessert.

The preparation of the *pastelitos* requires some patience and care. The pastry is repeatedly coated with fat, folded and rolled out once more. The goose fat, mixed with vegetable oil, has a fine flavor that gives an aroma to the *pastelitos*. To cook them successfully, the oil for deep-frying must not be too hot. In order to give them their characteristic shape, take two forks and separate the individual layers of pastry.

In Tangier's Jewish community, the ground beef filling is known as *miga*. Its special flavor is due to nutmeg, a spice that originates in the Moluccan Islands and has a strong, slightly sweetish taste. The scarlet husk surrounding the core with its nut is also used. Nutmegs are pressed, dried in the sun and then ground into powder or chopped into flakes known as mace. Its taste is reminiscent of cinnamon and pepper.

Turmeric, a reed-like plant, is widely used in Middle Eastern cuisine. The best quality comes from Bengal. The spice, sometimes known as "Indian saffron," has a slightly bitter taste and is also used to color dishes. It is excellently suited to the seasoning of ingredients that need to be simmered for a long time, as this is the only way it can develop its full aroma.

Pastelitos de ojas are served as a hot appetizer, best of all at the start of a festive meal.

For the filling, place the ground beef with the grated onion, chopped parsley, bay leaves, mace, nutmeg, and turmeric in a pot and season with salt and pepper. Cover with water and cook until the meat is done.

For the dough, break the eggs into a bowl. Add 6 tbsp/90 ml of oil, 6 tbsp/90 ml of water, salt and baking soda. Gradually add 3 1/8 cups/360 g flour and knead with your fingers. Continue kneading the mixture until it forms a dough.

Melt the goose fat and mix with 7 tbsp/ 100 ml of oil. Roll out the dough with a rolling pin on a floured surface. Brush it with the goose fat and oil mixture and dust with flour.

de Ojas

Fold the dough over in 3 equal sized layers. Turn the dough, roll out again and once again spread with oil and fat and dust with flour. Repeat these stages another 4 times.

Roll the dough out to make a rectangle. Place 3 balls of meat filling on the dough along the short side of the rectangle. Fold the dough over to cover the meat. Press the edges down around the meatballs. Cut and dust with flour. Make all the envelopes in this manner.

Heat the oil for deep-frying and put in the pastelitos. Using two forks, draw apart the dough layers a little, so the individual layers can be seen. Arrange the pastelitos on a serving plate.

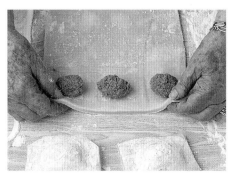

Small Passover

Preparation time: 40 minutes
Cooking time: 40 minutes
Difficulty: ★

Serves 4

3¼ lbs/1.5 kg   potatoes (Bintje if available)
½   unwaxed lemon
1 tsp   sugar
1 pinch   ground cinnamon
5   eggs
¼ cup/50 g   matzo flour or fine semolina
   oil for frying

For the filling:

1   onion
2¼ lbs/1 kg   ground beef
1 tsp   vegetable oil
½ bunch   parsley
2   bay leaves
½ tsp   grated nutmeg
½ tsp   mace
1   pinch saffron threads
   salt and pepper

The Passover festival commemorates the exodus of the Israelites from Egypt and the end of their enslavement. This important festival in the Jewish calendar is celebrated by all families. In remembrance of the event as told in the Torah, Jews, just the same as their forebears, may not eat anything made of leavened dough during the festival.

For the Passover festival, all the rooms of the house are thoroughly cleaned to remove the last particle of yeast, *hamets*. The ritual prescribes the eating of only unleavened bread or *matzo* at the table.

In Morocco, members of Tangier's Jewish community customarily serve little parmentiers at the Passover table. For these, they shape mashed potatoes, prepared without any milk products, into little domes. With their delicious filling of ground beef, onion, nutmeg, mace, bay leaves, oil, salt, and pepper, they are particularly popular with children.

This very filling Tangier specialty is more than a substitute for unleavened bread. For Passover, the semolina is replaced with matzo flour, ground from grain that has not been in contact with water, and is often used during the festival.

The best type of potato for the mashed potatoes is "Bintje." This yellow, oval variety can be found in season from September to May. Whatever you use, the parmentiers should not be fried until shortly before serving.

The parmentiers are redolent of mace, a little-used spice made from the scarlet husk of the nutmeg that is pressed and dried and sold as powder or in fine flakes.

For the filling, peel and grate the onion. Chop the parsley. Peel the potatoes for the parmentiers and cook them in salted water. Wash the half lemon, grate the peel and put aside.

Heat the ground beef with 1 tsp of oil, then pour on water to cover. Add parsley, onion, bay leaves, nutmeg, mace, and saffron threads. Season with salt and pepper. Cook until all the water has evaporated.

Mash the cooked potatoes. Add grated lemon peel, sugar, and ground cinnamon. Knead the mixture with your hands. Boil 2 eggs in salted water, shell and put aside.

Parmentiers

Use your hands to make ball shapes out of the mashed potatoes. Hollow these out to form bowls.

Chop the hard-boiled eggs. Fill the shells of mashed potatoes with ground beef and place a piece of egg on top of each. Shape the mashed potato bowls into cones.

Break 3 eggs and beat them. Dip the parmentiers first in egg, then in matzo flour or semolina. Heat the oil in a pan and deep-fry the parmentiers until light brown. Serve the parmentiers in little bowls.

Berber

Preparation time: 25 minutes
Cooking time: 30 minutes
Difficulty: ✳

Serves 4

3½ oz/100 g   tomatoes
2¾ oz/80 g   green and red bell
                 peppers
4½ oz/120g   zucchini
4½ oz/120 g   eggplant
2   onions

½ bunch   parsley
1 bunch   fresh cilantro (coriander)
2 cloves   garlic
1 tsp   paprika powder
3 tbsp/45 ml   olive oil
                 salt and pepper

The Sous region in the south of Morocco is well known for market gardening, especially vegetables. In earlier years, seasonal vegetables had to be eaten very quickly. For this reason, Berber women prepared a salad of eggplant, zucchini, tomatoes, and bell peppers. They also used the fine weather to preserve the valuable vegetables. They let them dry in the sun and then stored them in the house so that they could be used for couscous in the winter.

Today, Berber salad is served warm as an appetizer or as an accompaniment to couscous. This refreshing dish is easy to cook.

Eggplant, *the* summer vegetable par excellence, originated in India and has been eaten in Asia for more than 2,500 years. The best-known variety of eggplant is the one with deep violet, oval fruits. However, there are other varieties:

long ones, round ones, black ones and white ones. Eggplants are an essential component of many Middle Eastern and Mediterranean dishes where they are often combined with tomatoes, zucchini, olives, and garlic. Choose small eggplant fruits; the large ones are often full of hard seeds.

This is also true of zucchini. It is better to use small fruit that are firm at the ends. The cut mark on the stalk should be fresh. The larger the fruit, the less tender the flesh. The color should always be uniform. In this recipe, zucchini are used with their peel. The chef recommends rubbing them down lightly before cooking.

Tomatoes are thought to have originated in Peru. To make them easy to peel, score the tops and dip them into boiling water for a few minutes.

Pour boiling water over the tomatoes and peel them. Cut into thin slices. Cut red and green bell peppers, zucchini and eggplant into thin strips.

Cut the onions into thin rings. Chop parsley and cilantro. Crush the garlic.

Fry the onions in the oil until translucent. Add paprika powder; season with salt and pepper.

Salad

Add strips of zucchini, eggplant, and peppers. Pour on a little water. Simmer, covered, on a low heat for about 15 minutes.

Add slices of tomato.

Add parsley, cilantro, and garlic and cook for about another 10 minutes. Serve the Berber salad on salad plates.

Seafood

Preparation time: 20 minutes
Cooking time: 45 minutes
Difficulty: ✱

Serves 4

1½ lbs/650 g	mussels
1½ lbs/650 g	small shrimp
1	lemon
7 oz/200 g	black olives
	salt

For the chermoula sauce:

1 clove	garlic
1 bunch	parsley
1 bunch	cilantro (coriander)
½	pickled lemon
7 tbsp/100 ml	argan oil
2	fresh lemons
1 pinch	paprika
1 pinch	Moroccan saffron powder for coloring
1 pinch	ground cumin
	salt and black pepper

Nearly all Moroccan salads are made with either cooked or raw vegetables: *chachouka* is made with broiled (roasted) paprika, *zaalouk* with pickled eggplant or pickled pumpkin, and there are also potato salads, beet salads, or carrot salads. For this dish the chef would like to introduce you to a very sophisticated cold entrée; mussels and shrimp cooked in a fine *chermoula* sauce.

In Morocco a great variety of shrimp is available in the markets, but the ones most used are the medium-sized common shrimp. Most of the crustaceans with which the entire country is supplied are delivered to the ports of Agadir and Safi.

The seafood cooked in *chermoula* sauce can then be prepared in many different ways: mixed with Chinese thread noodles, they make a splendid filling for a *dorade*, but also for the famous Moroccan *briouates*.

You can even use them for a savory bake: in a baking dish, alternate layers of *yufka* pastry with the seafood *chermoula* and bake in the oven until golden-brown.

For this recipe, Abdelmalek al-Meraoui has chosen blue mussels. These fat, fleshy mussels are the best currently available in Morocco.

Argan oil comes from the south-west of the country. This is produced from the fruit of the argan tree. The nuts in the fruit flesh are three times as thick as hazel nuts and very hard to crack. The oily "almonds" within are smaller than sunflower seeds.

Peel the garlic. Chop together with parsley, cilantro, and pickled lemon.

Steam the mussels or place them in boiling water until they open. Pour on cold water to stop the cooking process. Remove the mussel flesh. Poach the shrimp in cold water to which lemon slices have been added and then shell them.

Put a little argan oil into a pan. Add parsley, cilantro, garlic, half a pickled lemon, and fresh, pressed lemon juice and stir until a chermoula is created.

with Chermoula

Season the chermoula with salt and pepper. Add paprika, Moroccan saffron, and cumin. Cook for 10 minutes, stirring.

Add shrimp to the chermoula. Fry briefly, stirring.

Add mussels to the sauce and mix in. Cook for 15 minutes and then allow to cool. Serve the salad in little bowls, garnished with pieces of black olives. Serve cold.

Spinach Salad

Preparation time: 30 minutes
Cooking time: 25 minutes
Difficulty: ★

Serves 4

4½ lbs/2 kg	fresh leaf spinach
7 tbsp/100 ml	argan oil
1 bunch	parsley
1 bunch	cilantro (coriander)
1 clove	garlic
1 pinch	saffron threads

1 pinch	ground cumin
1 pinch	paprika
1	pickled lemon
9 oz/250 g	fresh tomatoes
7 oz/200 g	red olives
	salt and pepper

Salads with argan oil are popular all over Morocco. In the country, they are often made with the leaves of the mallow plant, which grows wild in hedgerows and along the roadside. In restaurants, on the other hand, cooks like to use fresh spinach which can easily be bought in the market. This spinach salad is an excellent winter appetizer; Abelmalek al-Meraoui serves it cold.

Spinach, a vegetable that is widely available all over the world, is eaten rarely in Morocco. If it is served at table, it is usually in the form of a salad or a garnish, for example, for rice dishes. The chef here emphasizes the spinach flavor by serving it with *chermoula* sauce. The salad can be further varied by adding finely diced white fish (bream, rockling, John Dory, or similar), shrimp or small pieces of beef or lamb.

Argan oil gives this salad its particular flavor, typical of the plain of Sous not far from Agadir in the south-west of Morocco. The oil is produced in the mountains of the Anti-atlas, by families still using traditional methods. It takes the women some 15 hours of hard work to produce four cups (one liter) of oil.

First of all, the fruits of the argan tree are harvested and dried. They are then crushed to separate the kernel from the fruit flesh. Then comes the most laborious stage: each kernel is cracked open between two stones to free the little seeds within it. The seeds are toasted, giving them a nutty flavor, and then ground between millstones. The resulting paste is kneaded with lukewarm water and finally, pressed. 220 lbs (100 kilograms) of dried fruit produce an average of 13 cups (3.3 liters) of oil.

Wash the spinach under running water and then chop coarsely with a knife. Steam for around 10 minutes and then allow to cool.

Use your hands to press out the slightly cooled spinach leaves over a bowl, removing as much moisture as possible.

For the chermoula, put argan oil, chopped parsley, and chopped cilantro, crushed garlic clove, salt, pepper, saffron, cumin, paprika, and small cubes of pickled lemon in a pan. Allow to simmer on the stove, stirring.

with Argan Oil

Pour boiling water over 7 oz/200 g tomatoes and skin, halve them and remove seeds. Cut the fruits into quarters and chop them. Also chop the olives.

When the chermoula is well simmered, add the chopped tomatoes. Allow to simmer for around 5 minutes, stirring.

Add the chopped spinach to the chermoula. Bring to the boil on a high heat, stirring. Finally, add the chopped olives. Garnish the salad with the remaining tomatoes and serve as cold as possible.

Salad of

Preparation time:	30 minutes
Cooking time:	45 minutes
Difficulty:	★

Serves 5

2¼ lbs/1kg	tomatoes
½ tsp/2 g	fine salt
1 pinch	Moroccan saffron powder for coloring
¼ tsp	saffron threads
5 or 6	cinnamon sticks

2¼ cups/500 g	sugar
7 tbsp/100 ml	orange flower water
⅘ cup/200 ml	peanut oil

The fields and greenhouses of Morocco produce fresh tomatoes all the year round. This amazing salad of fresh tomatoes is easy to prepare and it makes a welcome appetizer. Because of the sugar, the tomatoes turn an intensive red in color. In consistency and taste, they are reminiscent of a compote of dried apricots.

The Moroccans love to eat sweet tomatoes cold or warm as a salad, part of a selection of *kemias*. They are not only distinctive and decorative, but, with the sweet touch to their flavor, simply delicious. They can keep well for three to four days in the fridge. They are also used to garnish tagines of chicken with onions, cinnamon, and ginger.

It is necessary to know that the Moroccans have developed preserving food in the most diverse ways into an art. Red or black olives, lemons, little onions, small peppers, and bell peppers, but also beef (*le khlii*) are cooked and pickled using salt, but sweet sauces are preferred, using tomatoes, dried beans, plums, figs, pears, apples, and similar fruits. Particularly good for sweet preserves is a mixture of sugar and honey.

This appetizer will be most successful if you choose fine, round, deep-red tomatoes of medium size. The fruits should be quite firm and not too juicy, as liquid—in the form of orange flower water and oil—is added during the cooking. The tomatoes should still be fleshy after removing the skin and the seeds.

In Moroccan salads, you often find vegetables combined with orange flower water. Cucumbers, grated and preserved in white vinegar with sugar and orange flower water, are often included among *kemias*.

Remove stalk base from tomatoes. Cut a cross in the flesh at the other end. Blanch in boiling water. When the skin loosens, remove from the water with a slotted spatula.

Immediately place the tomatoes into a container with iced water. Carefully remove the skins with a knife.

Halve all the tomatoes vertically. Remove the seed cores, in one piece if possible.

Sweet Tomatoes

Place all the tomatoes onto a baking sheet, hollowed out side up.

Distribute salt, Moroccan saffron, saffron threads, and cinnamon sticks over the tomatoes.

Sprinkle with sugar, then drizzle over orange flower water, and peanut oil. Cover the tomatoes with a large piece of aluminum foil. Bake in the oven for 45 minutes at 300 °F/150 °C. Serve hot or cold.

Salad of Tomatoes

Preparation time:	*20 minutes*
Cooking time:	*15 minutes*
Difficulty:	★

Serves 4

14 oz/400 g	medium-sized tomatoes
4 tbsp/60ml	olive oil
6 oz/175 g	green bell peppers
6 oz/175 g	red bell peppers
½ bunch	fresh cilantro (coriander)
2 oz/50 g	fresh parsley
2 cloves	garlic

1 oz/25 g	pickled lemon
1 pinch	ground cumin
	oil for deep-frying
	salt and pepper

For the garnish:

2 oz/50 g	black olives
2	eggs
	fresh cilantro (coriander)

This refreshing salad with tomatoes and bell peppers is currently perhaps the most frequently served salad in Morocco. There are two types of salads: for *taktouka* the ingredients are cooked—fried tomatoes, bell peppers, zucchini, or eggplant are used according to preference, or salads are prepared using boiled carrots, potatoes, or sweet potatoes, seasoned with garlic and parsley. For raw salads, on the other hand, vegetables are simply cleaned and served with a sauce of olive oil and parsley.

When making this salad, you can choose between the broad, compact variety or smaller and longer bell peppers. Once they are cooked and chopped, their original appearance hardly matters. Nowadays you can buy bell peppers all year round, although they are actually in season from May to September. The ripe peppers are at first dark green in color, but with increasing ripeness they eventually become a deep red and their flavor is then much sweeter.

Moroccan agriculture also produces great quantities of excellent tomatoes: bush tomatoes, greenhouse tomatoes, plum, and cherry tomatoes, which can also be made into preserves when skinned. Moroccans particularly favor the regional Melsa variety with its large and very smooth fruits. These are just as suited to making raw or cooked vegetable salads as they are for preparing *harira*, the "national soup" of Morocco, essential for every Ramadan festive meal.

Some cubes of pickled lemon give additional aroma to the salad and enliven it with their strong yellow color. In June, the small *mkrad* and *beldi* lemons, with their flattened ends, are ready, and can be pickled in Mason jars, sprinkled with plenty of salt.

Remove the stalk end of the tomatoes and cut a cross in them. Blanch in boiling water. When the skin begins to loosen, take them out of the water with a slotted spatula. Place in a container of iced water and remove the skin. Dice the tomatoes.

Place the eggs for 10 minutes in boiling water to boil hard. Heat the oil in a pan. Place green and red bell peppers into the hot oil until the skin loosens. Allow to cool. Shell the hard-boiled eggs.

Remove the skin of the peppers. Cut them lengthways into 2 halves. Remove the pith and the seeds with the point of a knife. Dice the flesh finely.

and Bell Peppers

Chop parsley and cilantro finely on a board. Peel the garlic and also chop finely. Dice the pickled lemon into small cubes.

Mix diced bell peppers, chopped herbs, garlic, and diced lemon in a salad bowl. Season with salt and pepper and add pinch of cumin.

Add a dash of olive oil and mix all ingredients again. Arrange the salad on a serving plate. Garnish with halved olives, hard-boiled eggs, and small leaves of cilantro.

Kemia Salad,

Preparation time: 20 minutes
Cooking time: 40 minutes
Difficulty: ☆

Serves 4

For the eggplant purée:
2 each — eggplants, tomatoes
2 cloves — garlic
1 — onion
— olive oil, paprika, cumin

For the seafood salad:
3½ oz/100 g each — calamaries (small squid), meagre (or other white fish)
1 each — onion, lemon
— saffron, olive oil, salt, pepper

For the tomato and pepper salad:
— oil for deep-frying
2 each — peppers, tomatoes

5 stems each — cilantro (coriander), parsley
2 cloves — garlic
— cumin, olive oil, white vinegar, salt, pepper

For the cucumber salad:
1 each — cucumber, tomato
4 stems — parsley

1 — onion
— cumin, olive oil, white vinegar, salt, pepper

For the zucchini salad:
1 each — zucchini, onion
2 cloves — garlic
— saffron, paprika, olive oil

For the bell pepper salad:
2 each — yellow peppers, red peppers, onions
2 cloves — garlic
8 stems — parsley
2 tbsp/30 ml — olive oil
— salt and pepper

For the carrot salad:
2 — carrots
4 stems — parsley
4 stems — cilantro (coriander)
1 tbsp/15 ml — white vinegar
— paprika, cumin, olive oil, salt, pepper

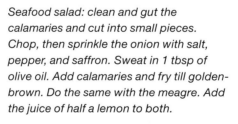

Most Moroccans would never receive guests without offering them a selection of fresh and colorful *kemias*, which are served on small plates. The host will arrange the little *kemia* dishes around the table and place the hot dish in the middle. While enjoying the main course, the guests can, just as they wish, help themselves to this or that salad with a small spoon. The indispensable flat, round Moroccan bread is served as an accompaniment.

This ensemble of different salads displays the variety of Moroccan garden vegetables, although it was not until the 16th century that the conquistadors brought tomatoes, chiles, bell peppers, and zucchini from America. The eggplant had long been enjoyed in India and Persia before it reached Morocco in the 15th century.

In our salad, the chef chops the raw calamaries before frying them in oil. They can, however, equally well be poached in boiling water with a dash of lemon juice. Immediately after cooking, immerse the calamaries in ice water to keep them tender. The meagre, a large fish with very delicate flesh, belongs to the croaker family. They are caught in the Atlantic and in the Mediterranean.

As is the case with the cuisine in every part of the Mediterranean, Moroccan cooking is also very strongly influenced by the flavor of olive oil, made from a great variety of types of olive and available in many different qualities. In the traditional oil press, the fruits are crushed by a thick millstone, usually powered by a donkey or a horse.

Eggplant purée: poach the eggplant with tomatoes, garlic, and onions. Purée in a blender until a paste is formed. Fry on a low heat in 2 tbsp of olive oil with a pinch of paprika and cumin.

Seafood salad: clean and gut the calamaries and cut into small pieces. Chop, then sprinkle the onion with salt, pepper, and saffron. Sweat in 1 tbsp of olive oil. Add calamaries and fry till golden-brown. Do the same with the meagre. Add the juice of half a lemon to both.

Tomato and bell pepper salad: fry peppers, skin them and chop. Scald the tomatoes, peel and chop. Finely chop cilantro, parsley, and garlic. Mix tomatoes, peppers, parsley, cilantro, salt, pepper, a pinch of cumin, garlic, olive oil, and vinegar.

Earth and Sea

Cucumber and zucchini salads: mix diced cucumber and tomato with chopped parsley, onion, cumin, salt, pepper, olive oil, and vinegar. Dice the zucchini. Fry the chopped onion and garlic in 2 tbsp of oil. Add diced zucchini, saffron, and paprika.

Bell pepper salad: chop 1 onion and 1 clove of garlic and fry in olive oil. Lightly fry the red bell pepper and sprinkle with half the chopped parsley. Prepare the yellow bell pepper salad in the same way.

Carrot salad: cut the carrots into sticks and poach in salt water. Drain. Mix the carrots with salt and pepper, 1 pinch paprika and cumin, chopped parsley and cilantro, vinegar and olive oil. Serve all salads fresh.

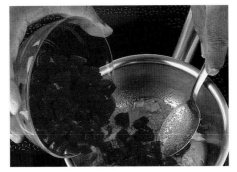

Cucumber Salad

Preparation time: 15 minutes
Difficulty: ★

Serves 4

1 ⅛ lbs/500 g	cucumbers
1 bunch	fresh thyme
½ cup/100 g	sugar
1 tbsp	orange flower water

For the garnish (as desired):
½ bunch   fresh mint
             ground cinnamon

This cucumber salad with fresh thyme makes an extraordinarily refreshing appetizer. The summery recipe is especially popular in Fez. The salad is easy to prepare and also very original, because the savory thyme blends harmoniously with the sugar and the delicate aroma of the orange flower water.

Like zucchini, cucumbers are the fruits of an all-the-year-round plant of the pumpkin family. They originated in the Himalayas and have pale green, crunchy and fresh fruit flesh. Cucumbers contain a great deal of water and only a few calories; on the other hand, they are a useful source of vitamin C.

The fleshy, firm, and cylindrical fruits almost always need to be peeled, as the peel is often bitter. The variety used by the chef comes from a greenhouse. Greenhouse cucumbers can vary in size, but always have a smooth skin and are available all the year round. Garden-grown cucumbers often have warty skins and thick seeds. It is strongly recommended that you try the cucumbers first to avoid the salad turning out bitter.

For his recipe, Abdellah Achiai has chosen exclusively regional ingredients. The thyme used is a variety that grows wild in the Atlas range. The Atlas Mountains with their breathtaking landscape are named after the famous Titan of Greek mythology. The thyme that grows there has a unique aroma. The Moroccans ascribe thousands of qualities to the herb, including the capacity to strengthen the organism. You can also make this appetizer using ordinary thyme.

This wonderfully light salad is particularly delicious when eaten in hot weather.

Peel the cucumbers with a vegetable peeler and keep 3 to garnish the plates.

Grate the cucumbers finely.

Cut the cucumbers reserved for garnish into thin slices.

with Atlas Thyme

Rub the thyme between your fingers over a plate.

To make the salad dressing, put thyme, sugar, and orange flower water into a bowl.

Add the grated cucumbers to the dressing and mix together. Arrange the salad in the middle of a plate and garnish with cucumber slices, mint and cinnamon (if used).

R'jla Salad with

Preparation time:	20 minutes
Cooking time:	35 minutes
Difficulty:	★

Serves 6

6 bunches	*r'jla*
3 bunches	flat-leaf parsley
2 bunches	fresh cilantro (coriander)
⅔ oz/20 g	garlic
⅔ oz/20 g	sweet paprika
1 oz/25 g	cayenne pepper
	salt and pepper

2 tbsp/30 ml	olive oil
9 oz/250 g	pickled red olives
2	pickled lemons

Moroccan gourmets have a particular liking for salads made from fresh, colorful vegetables or herbs that are readily available in the country. M'hamed Chahid has put together a very original creation based on a wild plant named *r'jla* and flavored with cilantro, parsley, cayenne pepper, and paprika. He also uses the same recipe for mallow, a spring plant often found in cornfields and by the roadside. Out of season, it is best to use Swiss chard or spinach leaves. The salad will then look a little different, as the spinach will collapse after steaming, while mallow and *r'jla* keep their shape better in cooking.

R'jla is always used in salads and belongs to the purslane family. The leaves have a slightly sour, sharp taste. The stalk is fairly thick, striped pale green and red. The stalks bear bushes of thick, smooth, teardrop-shaped leaves, a little less than an inch long and about half an inch wide. *R'jla* grows in wheatfields and vineyards in the spring and summer and is not sold in the markets in Morocco. However, children can be seen offering it for sale to passing drivers along the roadside.

After cooking, the chef garnishes his dish with pickled red olives. The olive fruit, a virtual symbol of Mediterranean countries, goes through several stages of ripeness. At first they are green, they then become red. With increasing ripeness they become purple and finally black. After harvesting, the red olives are kept in a broth of salt, vinegar and lemon juice for a long time to preserve them. They go wonderfully well with pickled lemons.

Wash the r'jla stems under running water. Cut off smaller stalks with their leaves.

Place several stems onto a cutting board and chop coarsely with a knife.

Bring water to the boil in a couscous steamer. When it is bubbling, place the chopped r'jla in the strainer part of the steamer and place it above the boiling water. Cover. As soon as the steam rises, steam, covered, for 20 minutes.

Lemons and Olives

Chop parsley, cilantro, and garlic. Fry garlic lightly in a pan with a little oil. Season with salt and pepper. Add paprika and cayenne pepper.

Add parsley and cilantro to the pan. Cook for 5 minutes on high heat, stirring.

Finally, add the steamed r'jla to the mixture. Cook for another 5–6 minutes. Add the olives, pits removed. Allow to cool. Decorate with olives and strips of pickled lemon and then serve.

Soups

Soup with

Preparation time: 40 minutes
Cooking time: 40 minutes
Difficulty: ☆

Serves 4

4	pigeons, each 1 lb/450 g
1	egg white
3½ oz/100 g	carrots
2	onions
3½ oz/100 g	leeks
3½ oz/100 g	celery sticks
½ bunch	fresh parsley
½ bunch	fresh cilantro (coriander)
2 tbsp/30 ml	vegetable oil

1 tsp	yellow food coloring (as desired)
3½ oz/100 g	noodles for soup
	salt and pepper

For the stock:

1 stem	thyme
1	bay leaf
1 clove	garlic
1 stick	celery
2 stems	parsley
2 stems	cilantro (coriander)
	salt and pepper

For the garnish:

	parsley

When winter comes, the people of Fez warm themselves with *shorba* containing pigeon meatballs and vegetables. This delicious traditional soup makes a good main course.

Pigeons are much favored by Moroccans. They have delicate flesh with a very fine flavor. This bird is considered a luxury dish and can be found in the markets from spring to summer. Wild pigeons are definitely preferable to the domesticated variety. If you have problems removing the pigeon breast meat, ask your butcher to do it, but don't forget to keep the wings and carcasses for the stock.

The intense aroma of *shorba* is mostly due to the stock. This is made from the pigeon carcasses, cilantro, parsley, thyme, bay leaf, garlic, and celery.

Shorba contains plenty of vegetables and is rich in vitamins. The leeks develop their gentle, slightly sweetish aroma particularly well if cut into small cubes. Leeks originate in the Middle East and are a cultivated form of garlic.

The white part of the leeks, which is favored in use, gives the dish a wonderful flavor. Clean the leeks thoroughly, as sand and earth are often caught between the leaves. To keep leeks for a longer period, do not cut them small first.

Abdellah Achiai adds noodles to thicken the soup. He uses a very fine pasta, known as *chaaria* in Morocco, that gives the soup a firmer consistency. This exquisite *shorba* with its pigeon meatballs and vegetables is a treat to indulge the palates of even the most choosy gourmet.

Clean and gut the pigeons, bone and remove the breast meat. Keep the carcasses for stock.

Remove the skin of the breast and cut the meat into small cubes. Grind in a food processor. Mix the meat with the egg white. Keep cool.

For the stock, place the carcasses, thyme, bay leaf, clove of garlic, celery, parsley, and cilantro in a pan. Cover with water, season with salt and pepper. Cook the stock for some 20 minutes and then put through a sieve.

Pigeon Meatballs

Peel the carrots and onions and dice very finely. Do the same with the leeks and celery. Wash the parsley and cilantro and chop very finely.

Sweat the vegetables, chopped parsley and chopped cilantro in the oil. Add the stock and food coloring as desired. Cook for about 15 minutes. Use your hands to form small meatballs from the meat and egg mixture.

Add the noodles and the meatballs to the soup. Cook for about 5 minutes, then taste and adjust seasoning. Pour the shorba into plates and garnish with chopped parsley.

Mediterranean

Preparation time:	*20 minutes*
Cooking time:	*35 minutes*
Difficulty:	☆

Serves 4

7 oz/200 g	white fish fillets
7 oz/200 g	shelled shrimp
3½ oz/100 g	button mushrooms
2	onions
4 cloves	garlic
7 oz/200 g	calamaries (small squid)
¼ tsp/1 g	saffron threads
1 tbsp/15ml	olive oil

1 tbsp/15 ml	peanut oil
2	fresh tomatoes
4 tbsp	tomato paste
3½ oz/100 g	thin soup noodles
1 bunch	parsley
1 bunch	cilantro (coriander)
1 tbsp	cornstarch
	salt and pepper

Moroccan cuisine includes a great variety of soups, all under the name of *shorba*. There should always be some chopped ingredients in the thick, aromatic stock.

Here, Bouchaïb Kama introduces us to a recipe from the Mediterranean coast, in which he uses seafood and white fish. In Arabic, the soup is known as *shorba belhout*. When it comes to *shorba*, there is no limit to the imagination of Moroccan cooks: *harira* is made with tomatoes, coriander, and lamb, and then there are *shorbas* with vegetables, noodles, and poultry, with shrimp, button mushrooms, soup noodles, and cilantro and so on. There is even a "white *shorba*" made from semolina cooked in salt water, mixed with milk and flavored with olive oil.

Nearly all kinds of fish and seafood can be used for this Mediterranean *shorba*. Morocco's coastline, along the Atlantic and the Mediterranean, is 2,175 miles (3,500 kilometers) long. The country therefore has a huge area available for catching fish and for profits from intensive deep-sea fishing. From the Atlantic waters jumbo shrimp, tuna, and turbot come onto the market, while in the Mediterranean the catch is mainly bream or swordfish.

Many different kinds of shrimp compete for the esteem of Moroccan gourmets. The Mediterranean varieties, however, are far smaller than their Atlantic cousins. For this *shorba*, you can also use cockles, scallops, or blue mussels.

In Morocco, soup is accompanied by the traditional flat wheatmeal bread. In earlier times, this bread was prepared in the following manner: an earthenware container, the *farrah*, was placed in a hole dug in the ground. The bread was baked brown in the *farrah* under a platter covered with embers.

Dice the fish fillets, shelled shrimp, button mushrooms, onions, and garlic very finely. Cut off the heads of the calamaries, draw out the intestines and the bone, and remove the skin. Turn the mantle inside out like a glove, rinse, and chop.

In a pan, briefly fry the cubes of onion and garlic sprinkled with saffron in the peanut and olive oil. Add the calamaries. Fry for 3–4 minutes, adding a little water. Season with salt and pepper.

Add the fish, diced shrimp, and button mushrooms. Mix and bring to the boil.

Fish Soup

Scald the fresh tomatoes, skin them, and chop finely. Mix the tomato paste in a bowl with water and add to the soup. Also add the chopped tomatoes. Cook for 10 minutes on medium heat.

Add the soup noodles and the chopped parsley and chopped cilantro. Taste and adjust seasoning. Cook for a further 5 minutes.

Mix the cornstarch with water in a small bowl. Pour into the soup and stir while on the heat until the soup thickens a little. Serve the soup in a handsome soup tureen.

Soup with

Preparation time:	15 minutes
Cooking time:	35 minutes
Difficulty:	★

Serves 4

2¼ lbs/1 kg	sea bass
7 oz/200 g	onions
7 oz/200 g	fennel bulb
3½ oz/100 g	celery sticks
1 bunch	flat-leaf parsley
1 bunch	cilantro (coriander)

1¾ sticks/200g	butter
½ tsp	ground nutmeg
10 cups/2.5 l	fish stock
6 cloves	garlic
½ tsp	salt
1 tsp	pepper

This *shorba* or soup from sun-drenched Essaouira is valued everywhere where fresh fish are unloaded by the fishermen. The originality of this sea bass soup lies in its spiciness: the powerful aroma of nutmeg and the slightly aniseed-like flavor of the fennel.

The making of the *shorba* can vary just as much as that of the bouillabaisse of Marseilles. The flavor differs somewhat if sea bass is replaced by allis shad, a less common fish living in the estuary waters of the rivers. You can in fact find allis shad all the year round in Rabat or Salé, two towns on the banks of the Bou Regreg, which flows into the Atlantic.

Whether you use sea bass or allis shad, the fish is cooked in a sauce or fried in a pan and then served with *chermoula*, a sauce made of oil, vinegar, cilantro, cumin, and mild or hot red paprika. You can do without the fish stock, but it is not hard to obtain ready-to-use stock in stores. Ideally, you prepare it in larger quantities yourself and keep it in the fridge. It makes a fine supplement to bouillon.

If the dish is prepared using allis shad, the cooking time is a little longer. Sea bass should not cook for longer than five minutes. Its flesh breaks apart very quickly and in any case it tastes better while still firm.

Before you start preparing the soup, prepare some garlic cream. Cook six unpeeled garlic cloves until they are soft. Then peel them and crush them in a little olive oil. Season with salt and stir until a cream is formed; you can simply add this to the soup shortly before serving.

Remove the scales from the fish and rinse under cold water. Slice into thick pieces and drain in a colander.

Peel the onions and clean the fennel. Dice finely, and do the same to the celery sticks. Chop parsley and cilantro. Keep each ingredient in a small bowl.

Melt some butter in a pot and then lightly fry parsley, cilantro, onions, and celery. Brown for 5 minutes on a low heat, stirring from time to time.

Sea Bass and Fennel

Add fennel to the pot and stir with a wooden spatula. Season with salt and pepper and sprinkle with nutmeg. Continue to cook for a further 5 minutes on medium heat, stirring constantly.

Add the fish stock and continue to cook on a medium heat for a further 20 minutes.

Finally, put the fish pieces into the pot and cook for a maximum of 5 minutes—the flesh should not break apart.

Harira with

Preparation time: 15 minutes
Soaking time: overnight
Cooking time: 1 hour 45 minutes
Difficulty: ☆

Serves 8

1¼ cups/200 g	garbanzo beans (chickpeas)
2 oz/50 g	rice
1 bunch	parsley
1 bunch	fresh cilantro (coriander)
1	onion
3½ oz/100 g	celery sticks
7 tbsp/100 ml	oil

5 oz/150 g	chicken breast fillets
2 envelopes	Moroccan saffron powder for coloring
1 cube	chicken stock
9 oz/250 g	tomato paste
6	eggs
⅞ cup/100 g	flour
	salt and pepper

For serving:

	lemons
	dried figs

During Ramadan, the powerful aroma of *harira*, which is made in all households, wafts through the streets. It is eaten as soon as the fast is broken, immediately after sunset. Moroccans always eat it accompanied by dried dates or figs and various small pastries.

This nourishing soup is made from pulses and flavored with cilantro, parsley, and tomato. It can be enriched according to taste by small pieces of lamb or chicken or meatballs (*kefta*), or simply cooked with a bone to give the bouillon more flavor. The soup is thickened with flour that has first been mixed with water. According to the customs of the region, soup noodles, rice, or eggs are also added.

In Morocco, pulses are a popular winter food, especially in the rough mountain climate. Dried garbanzo beans, lentils,

and beans are then on the daily menu. Like all beans, garbanzo beans ripen in their husks. Fresh garbanzo beans have a rather boring taste, and for this reason, almost the whole harvest is dried before being used as food.

In his restaurant, M'hamed Chahid generally uses short-grain rice for his stew. The rice is grown in the fertile Garb region (near Khénitra).

If the eggs are put into the pot towards the end of the cooking time, they don't need to cook for long. They will continue to cook in the soup when the pan is taken off the heat.

Squeeze the lemon directly before serving and add the juice to the soup or serve it separately. Strings of dried figs are decorative and make a wonderful sweet accompaniment.

Soak the garbanzo beans the evening before cooking. Cook the rice for 20 minutes in salted water. Finely chop the parsley and cilantro. Peel the onion and dice into small pieces. Do the same with the celery.

Heat the oil in a large pot. Lightly fry the finely diced ingredients, stirring. Add the drained garbanzo beans and the diced chicken breast meat.

Add saffron powder, salt, pepper, 1 crumbled chicken stock cube and tomato paste. Pour on 6 cups/1.5 l water, bring to the boil and simmer for 1 hour.

Rice and Figs

Mix the flour with water in a small bowl. Pour into the pot and, with the pot on the heat, stir in well to bind the soup. Allow to thicken for about 15 minutes.

At the end of the cooking time, add the cooked and drained rice to the soup.

Break the eggs into a bowl and add to the soup. Cook for 2–3 minutes, then take the pot from the heat. Serve with wedges of lemon and dried figs.

Fez Ramadan

Preparation time:	35 minutes
Soaking time:	12 hours
Cooking time:	1 hour 40 minutes
Difficulty:	✲

Serves 4

½ cup/100 g	yellow lentils
1¼ cups/200 g	garbanzo beans (chickpeas)
2	onions
1 bunch	cilantro (coriander)
1 bunch	parsley
1 stick	celery
9 oz/250 g	shin of beef
5	tomatoes

1 tsp	smen (preserved butter) or olive oil if not available
1 tsp	Moroccan saffron powder for coloring
1 tsp	ground ginger
1 cube	chicken stock
3½ oz/100 g	Greek noodles (kritharaki)
⅞ cup/100 g	flour
5 oz/150 g	tomato paste
	salt and pepper

For the garnish:

8	dates
8	figs (as desired)
	lemon (as desired)

It is impossible to imagine the heritage of Moroccan cuisine without *harira*. This traditional soup, made from meat, garbanzo beans, lentils, tomatoes, and celery, is eaten by every family during Ramadan. It is also served to a newly-married bride on the morning after the wedding night.

This nourishing dish, which can perhaps be compared to a Hungarian goulash, varies from region to region and family to family. However, for many Moroccans, the true *harira* is the one eaten in Fez. This royal city, with a culinary tradition going back fourteen centuries, is an upholder of tradition and has brought recipes to Moroccan cuisine that are worthy of their reputation. *Fassia* gastronomic culture is considered noble and elite and is distinguished by its skill and refinement.

This *harira* is easy to prepare and displays a subtle mixture of different aromas. It is therefore essential to cook it for a long time. Celery, *krafece* in Moroccan, gives soups, sauces, and ragouts a wonderful aroma, and is available all year round in the markets. Choose green sticks without wilted patches and no yellowish stains at the bulb end. They keep well in the fridge.

Harira fassia is unthinkable without lentils and garbanzo beans. Garbanzo beans, which originate in western Asia, develop a light nutty flavor. They are very nourishing and keep their shape when cooking. Don't forget to soak them for twelve hours and pull off the little husk that surrounds them. *Harira* is always eaten with a sweet accompaniment such as dates or figs.

Soak the lentils and the garbanzo beans the evening before cooking. Remove the husks from the garbanzo beans. Peel the onions and chop finely. Chop cilantro, parsley, and celery.

Dice the beef into small cubes. Scald the tomatoes and peel them. Cut into small cubes, purée and put aside.

Sweat the onions in the smen. Add diced meat, saffron powder, and ginger. Season with salt and pepper. Dissolve the chicken stock cube in a glass of water and pour into the pan. Add the garbanzo beans. Bring all ingredients to the boil.

Soup

Pour on water. Add cilantro, parsley, and celery. Cook for about 30 minutes. Add the lentils and cook for a further 20 minutes. Stir in puréed tomatoes. Cover and cook for a further 20 minutes.

Add the noodles. Cook for about 5 minutes. Mix flour and tomato paste with water.

Pour in the mixture and allow all ingredients to cook, covered, for about 15 minutes, stirring occasionally. Pour into a soup tureen and serve with dates, figs, and lemon.

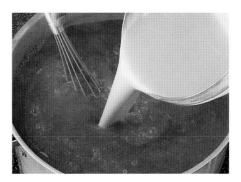

Vegetable Stew

Preparation time: 30 minutes
Cooking time: 45 minutes
Difficulty: ★

Serves 4

7 oz/200 g	shin of beef
3½ oz/100 g	onions
3 tbsp	oil
1 oz/30 g	flat-leaf parsley
3 oz/80 g	fresh cilantro (coriander)
2½ oz/75 g	celery sticks
¼ tsp	ground ginger

1 envelope	ground saffron
3½ oz/100 g	carrots
3½ oz/100 g	turnips
3½ oz/100 g	zucchini
2 oz/60 g	Greek noodles (*kritharaki*)
	salt and pepper

Here, Mohammed Aïtali presents a simple, economical stew, which is easy to make all year round. It includes Greek noodles and diced beef from the shin or shoulder. However, you can just cook a bone in the bouillon in order to give it more flavor. The stew can also be supplemented with lamb or poultry meat.

In Morocco, cattle are reared particularly in the fertile region around Meknès and around Fez, Doukhala, and in the mid-Atlas region. These animals are modest in size, weigh around 200–300 lbs, have a yellowish hide and do not produce large amounts of milk or meat. They are increasingly being replaced by foreign breeds that give better yields.

The stew, prepared with zucchini, carrots, onions, and turnips, can be enriched with finely chopped leeks or white cabbage. Don't add the zucchini to the sauce with the meat at the same time as the turnips and carrots—they will overcook.

The chef has used Greek noodles shaped like rice grains. They are made from durum wheat flour. The Moroccans didn't wait for the Italians in developing their own pasta. In Morocco, you can buy *mtafka* (soup noodles), *douida* (rice grains), *drihmat* (little squares), *fdaouch* (spaghetti), and *tarchta* (tagliatelle).

The Greek noodles must be cooked in very hot bouillon, as they will turn into a sticky dough if they are put into lukewarm or cold liquid. In Morocco, these noodles are also popular cooked in milk and eaten with butter and sugar. If you can't find Greek noodles, just use ordinary soup noodles.

Cut the boned beef into slices about ½ inch/1 cm thick and then into small, even cubes.

Peel the onions and chop them. Heat the oil in a large saucepan and brown the onions in it.

Add the cubed beef. Fry on a high heat and stir to avoid it sticking to the pan.

with Saffron

Add chopped parsley, chopped cilantro, and celery, together with ginger and saffron, to the pan. Fry for a few minutes. Season with salt and pepper. Cover with water and cook, covered, for about 20 minutes.

Peel the carrots and the turnips. Dice into little cubes of about $^1/_5$ inch/5 mm; do the same to the unpeeled zucchini. Add carrots and turnips to the sauce with the meat. Cook for 5 minutes, then add the zucchini and cook for another 5 minutes.

Add the Greek noodles to the very hot soup and cook for another 5 minutes on medium heat. Serve hot.

Bissara

Preparation time: 15 minutes
Cooking time: 30 minutes
Difficulty: ✶

Serves 4

9 oz/250 g	dried small beans
3	unpeeled cloves of garlic
2 tbsp/30 ml	olive oil
1 tsp	salt

For serving:

ground cumin
paprika
olive oil

In the winter, Moroccans like to warm themselves up with a plate of *bissara*. This intensively aromatic soup of dried beans, salt, and oil may seem a little dull in flavor at first, which is why each guest is provided with little bowls of olive oil, paprika, and cumin to flavor the soup according to taste.

Amina Khayar prepares *bissara* using very small dried beans, about the same size as peas. These have the advantage of cooking very quickly. Of course, the soup can also be prepared using fava beans or peas. Fresh fava beans go very well with pickled lemons, a combination frequently used in lamb tagines. There is also a couscous with green beans and wild figs, known as *kuran*. Small beans are popular poached and marinated in *chermoula* sauce. Dried beans, on the other hand, are always made into soups.

The beans must be rinsed several times to remove even the last traces of dirt. At the same time, this makes them lose some of their excess starch. Stir regularly during cooking to make the beans cook and break apart more quickly. The garlic you put into the soup can be peeled beforehand. Depending on the desired consistency, the soup can finally be passed through a sieve or puréed in a blender.

Amina Khayar's *bissara* also depends on the flavor of Moroccan olive oil. The best olive oil comes from the Berber regions in the south of the country. It is dark green in color and has a slightly bitter taste. In was not until King Hassan II commanded it that large-scale olive plantations were introduced to the country. These are cultivated to this day, covering an area of around 8,650 acres (3,500 hectares).

Pour the dried beans out onto a large plate or onto the work surface. Pick out bits of leaf, beans still in their husks, small stones etc. with your fingers.

Rinse the beans well in a bowl or in a colander under running water. Repeat at least 3 times in order to remove all impurities.

Put the beans into a large pot. Fill the pot three-quarters full with hot water.

Put the unpeeled garlic into the bean water. Add a generous splash of olive oil and season with salt. Cover and cook for 20–30 minutes.

Take the garlic out with a slotted spatula. Pour on cold water and then peel carefully with a small knife.

Put the bean soup and the garlic in a food processor and blend to a smooth purée. Taste and adjust seasoning. Serve hot with cumin, paprika, and olive oil to accompany.

Casbah

Preparation time:	20 minutes		1	onion
Cooking time:	25 minutes		1 tbsp/15 ml	olive oil
Difficulty:	☆		2 oz/50 g	Chinese thread noodles
			1	chicken stock cube
Serves 4			1 pinch	saffron threads
			4 tbsp/60 g	fine semolina
2	zucchini		1 tbsp	butter
2	carrots			salt and pepper
2	potatoes			
2	tomatoes			
½ bunch	cilantro (coriander)			
½ bunch	parsley			
2 cloves	garlic			

This vegetable soup was originally eaten in the "valley of the thousand *casbahs*," which lies along the route from er-Rachidia to Ouarzazate in southern Morocco. Almond and olive trees, cactus and reeds grow in this extraordinary landscape, and again and again one comes across one of the numerous *ksours*, castles built out of beaten clay.

In this region, the *casbah* culture has strongly influenced the local character. In earlier years, these mighty fortresses, originally rulers' residences, also served as safe refuges for the people of the villages when invasion threatened. In the *casbah*, the caravans trading between the Maghreb and the southern part of the African continent found a safe place to stay overnight, as well as a secure warehouse for their goods from distant lands.

According to legend it was the nomads who primarily enjoyed this fortifying soup of vegetables, noodles, and semolina. Today this popular dish is served mainly among the Berber families of Ouarzazate. It is easy to prepare and is usually served as a main course. The inhabitants of the region are particularly fond of noodles.

For this recipe, the chef has used Chinese thread noodles made from soy flour and available in long, mother-of-pearl-colored strands. They can be boiled or fried, and used in stews and fillings.

In earlier times, this vegetarian soup was made solely from seasonal vegetables. For example, for the zucchini it was necessary to wait until summer. Zucchini originate in Central and South America, but are now firmly established in Mediterranean cuisine. These vegetables are rich in water but are not overly filling. They should be an even green color.

Wash the zucchini. Peel the carrots and potatoes and grate the vegetables finely. Scald and chop the tomatoes.

Finely chop the cilantro and parsley. Peel and crush garlic cloves. Peel and finely chop the onion.

Lightly sweat the onion and garlic in a saucepan in olive oil. Cut up the thread noodles and add them. Also add the grated potatoes, carrots, and zucchini.

Vegetable Soup

Fill the pan three-quarters full of water. Add the stock cube.

Season with salt and pepper. Add saffron threads, parsley, and cilantro. Cook for about 20 minutes.

Add the semolina. Stir with a wooden spatula to bind the soup. Stir in the chopped tomatoes and the butter. Serve the casbah soup in little bowls.

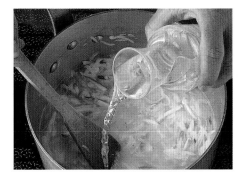

Sabbath Soup

Preparation time: 20 minutes
Soaking time: 12 hours
Cooking time: 5 hours
Difficulty: ✳

Serves 4

6 cups/1 kg	large garbanzo beans (chickpeas)
1 tsp	baking soda
2¼ lbs/1 kg	lean beef (shoulder and breast)
3	marrow bones

1	onion
1	potato
2 cloves	garlic
1 bunch	cilantro (coriander)
1 tsp	saffron threads
4 tbsp/60ml	vegetable oil
1 tsp	turmeric
	salt and pepper

Many of the Jews who come from Morocco nostalgically remember the garbanzo bean soup eaten on the evening before the Sabbath. This tasty dish is particularly popular today in Tangier and Meknès and is served on the Sabbath.

It is easy to make but needs some time to cook. In Judaism the use of fire is prohibited during the Sabbath. As a consequence, this specialty is prepared on the Friday afternoon. On the eve of the Sabbath, the family table resembles an altar. For the Jewish community, this is a privileged moment, to be experienced with joy, and also the opportunity of enjoying special dishes.

Garbanzo beans, highly esteemed everywhere in the Mediterranean countries, must be soaked for 12 hours in water before cooking. Victoria Berdugo also adds a teaspoon of baking soda to make them more digestible.

Garbanzo beans originate in Central Asia and are the fruits of a herb-like, annual plant. The pods contain three to four peas, which taste slightly nutty.

Garbanzo beans are very nourishing and keep their shape when cooking. While many Jews in Tangier prefer to crush or even purée them, whole peas, floating in the soup, are popular in Meknès.

This delicious soup contains a wonderful mixture of Middle Eastern aromas. Cilantro—coriander leaf—without which Moroccan cuisine would be unimaginable, gives the soup its characteristic touch. Cilantro is known as *kosbor* in Arabic. It develops the whole power of its flavor in this soup. In order to ensure that the garbanzo bean soup turns out really spicy, add some of the spices right at the end of cooking.

Put the garbanzo beans into boiling hot water (but not on the stove) the evening before. Add 1 tsp baking soda. Cover and soak for 12 hours.

Put the garbanzo beans in clear water the next day and rub them with your hands in order to release the skins.

Put the beef and the bones into a saucepan. Add garbanzo beans, onion, potato, crushed garlic cloves, a tied ½ bunch of cilantro, saffron threads, and oil. Fill the pan with water and cook, covered, for about 4½ hours.

with Garbanzo Beans

Take out the meat and the bones. Purée the garbanzo beans and the other ingredients in a blender.

Finely chop the other half of the bunch of cilantro. Add to the garbanzo bean soup with the turmeric. Taste and adjust seasoning with salt and pepper.

Replace the meat and bones in the soup. Cook for another 30 minutes or so. Take the bones out of the soup. Serve the garbanzo bean soup on plates and serve the meat separately.

Dchicha

Preparation time:	15 minutes
Cooking time:	40 minutes
Difficulty:	☆

Serves 4

1	onion
2 cloves	garlic
1 pinch	dried thyme
2 tbsp/30 ml	olive oil
7 oz/200 g	barley, crushed

| 2 cups/500 ml | milk |
| | salt and pepper |

For the garnish:

| | olive oil |

In Moroccan, *dchicha* refers to pounded barley. This winter soup is typical of the Central Atlas region and a fixed component of Berber cuisine.

This very popular *dchicha* soup is prepared according to a recipe that is particularly easy to follow. It is made from barley, garlic, thyme, onion, and olive oil and is eaten in the mornings or the evenings. It is often served to young mothers to restore their strength. In Moroccan culture, dishes based on a foundation of cereals such as wheat, barley, millet, or flour, including crepes, are highly regarded.

Dchicha, also known as *ibrine*, is especially esteemed among the Berbers. Barley has been cultivated and made into soups and gruels for thousands of years. You can, however, also make *dchicha* using polenta.

It is not possible to imagine the dish without the scent of garlic. Garlic belongs to the onion family and comes from Central Asia. It is famous for its medicinal powers. In spring, fresh garlic is found in the markets. It is very tasty, soft and easy to peel. But whether it is fresh or not, feel the bulb before you buy. It should always be firm and full.

Thyme is excellently suited to soups, eggs, meat, and broiled fish. This aromatic herb is native to the Mediterranean region and can be recognized by its small grayish-green leaves. Fresh or dried thyme can be used in the dishes. The aromatic scent of this perennial plant is very intensive thanks to the essential oil, thymol.

Dchicha is a country soup through and through. Before serving, you can give it a touch of color by drizzling on some olive oil.

Peel and chop the onion. Crush the garlic cloves.

Fry the chopped onion, crushed garlic, and dried thyme in olive oil in a saucepan.

Cover the mixture with water and stir with a wooden spatula.

Soup

When the mixture boils, add the crushed barley and cook for about 30 minutes.

Stir the soup with a wooden spatula to thicken it.

Add the milk. Bring to the boil and take the pan from the heat. Pour the dchicha soup into plates and drizzle with a little olive oil.

Tagines &
Couscous

Couscous with

Preparation time: 1 hour 30 minutes
Cooking time: 4 hours
Difficulty: ★★

Serves 8

6½ lbs/3 kg	onions
1 stick	cinnamon
2 cups/500 ml	vegetable oil
½ cup/100 g	sugar
2 tsp	saffron powder

6 cups/1 kg	golden raisins
⅓ oz/10 g	honey
1 bunch	flat-leaf parsley
1 bunch	cilantro (coriander)
4½ lbs/2 kg	beef (rump)
6 cups/1 kg	medium coarse semolina
	salt and pepper

This couscous, cooked with onions and raisins, is extremely delicious. This recipe is of Jewish origin but with a strong Moroccan influence and requires some time to prepare. It is mainly served at religious festivals.

The onions, cooked with sugar and honey, are a genuine oriental delicacy. Their fine aroma comes to perfection when combined with saffron and cinnamon.

Onions are used in many recipes, as a flavoring as well as a vegetable. The onion originates in north Asia and has been cultivated for more than 5,000 years. It gives a wonderful aroma to ragouts. Moroccan onions are especially known for their fine, sweet flavor.

For this recipe, we recommend that you use large, firm-fleshed onions, which should be undamaged and not sprouting.

If this dish is carefully prepared, the delicate aroma of saffron can also be detected. In Arabic, this spice is known as *sa'faran*. The name contains the root *asfar*, yellow. Saffron, the most expensive spice in the world, is cultivated in the south of Morocco. Every year, from October onwards, the fields of purple crocus blooms that produce saffron extend to the horizon. Two hundred thousand flowers are needed to make a single pound (500g) of saffron.

The raisins added to the onions in cooking are definitely nourishing. They are often used in Moroccan cuisine for flavoring.

The greatest difficulty in making this recipe lies in preparing the semolina. You must work in the oil and water by hand, and this stage in the process must be repeated between each steaming.

Peel the onions and set one aside. Cut the others into fine slices and put in a pot. Add cinnamon. When the onions begin to sweat, add 7 tbsp/100 ml oil, sugar, salt, and 1 tsp saffron. Cook for 2 hours.

Once the onions have lost their liquid, add raisins and honey to the pot. Cook for a further hour, then put aside. Bind parsley and cilantro into 1 bunch.

Put the beef into the couscous steamer. Add parsley and coriander, the reserved onion, cut into two halves, and the remaining saffron. Season with salt and pepper. Pour on ⅔ cup/150 ml oil and 8 cups/2 l of water. Cook for 4 hours.

Raisins and Onions

Moisten the semolina with water and rub it between the palms of your hands.

Carefully knead the semolina and add oil. Continue to rub between the palms of your hands.

Cook the semolina for 1 hour in the strainer of a couscous steamer and repeat the process of rubbing with oil and water 6 times. Arrange the couscous with the onions and the meat on a serving dish. Serve the meat broth separately.

Lobster Couscous

Preparation time: 50 minutes
Cooking time: 1 hour
Difficulty: ★★

Serves 4

3 tbsp/45 ml	oil
3 cups/500 g	fine semolina
1	onion
1 bunch	cilantro (coriander)
1 bunch	parsley

2 bunches	watercress
2	lobsters each 3⅓ lbs/1.5 kg
9 oz/250 g	spring onions
1¼ sticks/150 g	butter
1 pinch	ground ginger
2 cups/500 ml	cream
	salt and pepper

Lahoussine Bel Moufid has very close links to the culinary heritage of his home country. At the same time, he lets himself be inspired by regional characteristics to create dishes with a special sophistication. This great Moroccan chef is ever increasing the gourmet's pleasure with his new inventions. He always uses national dishes as the foundation for these and has created a repertoire of recipes in which Middle Eastern and Mediterranean aromas are delightfully combined.

Lobster couscous with watercress cream is a perfect example. The idea for this sophisticated dish came from the Atlas Mountains. The Berber region of Imouzzer des Ida is famed for the purity of its waters. The people there pick the watercress, which grows wild, mix it with cream and serve it as an accompaniment to couscous. To make the vegetarian couscous a bit more nourishing, the chef came up with the idea of adding crayfish from the local rivers.

In the end, he replaced the crayfish with lobster, an elite crustacean from the sea, highly esteemed by gourmets. Lobsters have a hard shell surrounding the abdomen, tasty firm white flesh. The first set of legs has developed into claws with plenty of muscle flesh. Remember to remove the stomach where the head meets the body and the intestines at the tail end. In the fishmongers, lobsters are always sold live. Before preparing them, you must immerse them head first in bubbling, boiling water, in order to kill them. Take the lobster out again after one or at maximum two minutes. According to taste and budget, you can use spiny lobster or crayfish.

The watercress should be a strong green color and fresh, with undamaged stems and leaves. Watercress can only be kept for one day in the fridge before it starts to fade. The plants should be thoroughly sorted through, washed, and drained.

With your hands, rub 3 tbsp of oil into the semolina and then work in a little water.

In a couscous steamer, heat water with finely chopped onion, and half the cilantro and parsley (chopped). Add salt. When the water boils, cook the semolina for 15 minutes in the strainer. Work in a little fluid. Cook for another 15 minutes. Repeat both stages once more.

Wash the watercress. Take the leaves off one bunch and crush them with a mortar and pestle. Strain the liquid from the couscous steamer and put aside.

with Watercress Cream

Split the cooked lobster lengthways, starting from the head, into 2 halves. Break open the claws. Peel the spring onions, chop, sweat with 7 tbsp/100 g butter. Add the remaining cilantro and parsley (chopped), with the ginger and crushed watercress. Season with salt and pepper.

Place the halves of lobster in the mixture. Add the liquid from the couscous steamer and cook for 5 minutes. Take out the lobster and put aside.

Add the cream and the bunch of watercress. Reduce the sauce to three-quarters of its volume. Replace the lobster. Stir the remaining butter into the semolina. Arrange the lobster couscous on a plate with the watercress cream.

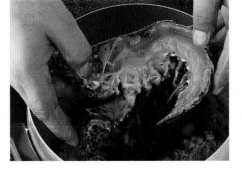

T'faya Couscous

Preparation time: 45 minutes
Cooking time: 1 hour 50 minutes
Difficulty: ★★

Serves 4

For the couscous:
2 cups/350 g	couscous semolina
2 tbsp/30ml	oil
	salt

For the chicken:
1	chicken, 2½ lbs/1.2 kg
10½ oz/300 g	onions
⅔ oz/20 g	flat-leaf parsley
⅔ oz/20 g	fresh cilantro (coriander)

1 pinch	ground ginger
2 pinches	saffron
7 tbsp/100 ml	olive oil
	salt and pepper

For the t'faya:
4	onions
2 tbsp/30 ml	olive oil
1¼ cups/200 g	golden raisins
¼ cup/50 g	sugar
1 tsp/5 g	ground cinnamon
¼ stick/30 g	butter
2 tsp/10 ml	orange flower water
	pepper

No Moroccan family would be able to manage without its couscous steamer. Everyone tries their hand at making the national dish, couscous. Mohammed Aïtali here introduces us to a variation using cooked chicken in a sauce made from onions, herbs, and saffron, served with *t'faya*, prepared from onions, raisins, and cinnamon. This couscous is a city dish and is most often prepared for wedding celebrations.

Each region of Morocco has its "own" traditional couscous recipe: *bidawi* is made with seven kinds of vegetables, the Berber couscous *belboula*, made from barley semolina, is made with meat, *sekkouk* features sour milk, couscous, fava beans and green figs, and there is also *medfoun*, a dish in which pigeons are hidden under the semolina.

The individual parts of the essential couscous steamer have different names: the lower part, in which the ingredients are cooked in a sauce or just in water, is known according to region as the *barma*, *tanjra*, or *marmita*. The strainer in which the couscous cooks is called *keskes*. The cloth tucked between both parts, sealing the join, is known as *kfal*. Today, most cooks use metal couscous steamers, though people in the country often still swear by their traditional earthenware ones.

Medium coarse durum wheat semolina is best for this couscous. There are three varieties of semolina to choose from in the shops: fine, medium, and coarse.

After jointing the chicken, rinse the pieces well under cold running water to remove blood and impurities. If the chicken begins to dry out or stick while cooking, add a little water and stir.

Joint the chicken. Separate the thighs first, then cut in two lengthways from the breast, cutting through the spine. Cut each half into 2 or 4 pieces. Rinse well under cold water and pat dry.

For the marinade, peel, and chop the onions and also chop the parsley and cilantro. Season with salt and pepper and adjust seasoning with 1 pinch ginger, saffron and a little olive oil.

Place the pieces of chicken in a pan after covering the bottom of the pan with oil. Fry for a few moments on high heat. Add the herb marinade and stir. Sprinkle on 1 pinch of saffron. Cook for 20–25 minutes.

with Chicken

Place the semolina in a bowl. Using your hands, work in a little olive oil and water. Cook 3 times for 20 minutes at a time in the strainer part, adding salt and more water between each stage.

For the t'faya, fry the chopped onions briefly in olive oil. Add raisins first, then cinnamon, pepper, and butter. Stir for a moment on high heat, then cover with water.

Flavor the t'faya with orange flower water. Cook for 15 minutes. Add the sugar halfway through the cooking. Arrange the couscous on a serving plate and place pieces of chicken and t'faya on top.

Dchicha

Preparation time: *1 hour*
Cooking time: *50 minutes*
Difficulty: ★★

Serves 6–8

1⅛ lbs/500 g	carrots
1⅛ lbs/500 g	turnips
1⅛ lbs/500 g	white cabbage
1⅛ lbs/500 g	zucchini
9 oz/250 g	pumpkin
1⅛ lbs/500 g	onions
4½ lbs/2 kg	*dchicha* (barley semolina)

2 cups/500 ml	argan oil
1	boned shank of veal
1 pinch	ginger
1 pinch	Moroccan saffron powder for coloring
1⅛ lbs/500 g	tomatoes
1 bunch	flat-leaf parsley
1 bunch	cilantro (coriander)
	salt and pepper

Cooks from Sous like to prepare *dchicha* with vegetables, thus creating an original and colorful couscous. The plain near Agadir is very fertile and famed for its cereals, vegetables and olive groves.

The name of this recipe is due to the semolina used for the couscous. The grains of *dchicha*, a barley semolina, are finely pounded. After steaming, the people of the Sous mix hot milk with the *dchicha* to make a gruel, or mix it with *lben*, soured milk. They also prize *barkouk*, a couscous served with honey or *amelou* sauce made from honey, almonds, and argan oil.

Argan oil, with its powerful scent, comes from the fruits of the argan tree, which grows wild. The fruits are yellow or beige and the size of olives. The argan tree grows to 25 or 30 feet, has a knotty trunk with numerous bulges and dense foliage. Argan trees can be found in the south-east of Morocco in isolated areas stretching north-west from Essaouira and up as far as the vale of Sous.

Giant pumpkins are also often used to enrich Moroccan couscous dishes. Their shape, whether elongated or round, is of no importance. What counts is their deep orange color. The best pumpkins come from the Doukhala region.

First of all, use your fingertips to knead a little lukewarm water into the semolina until all the grains are moistened and begin to swell. Only then should you add the argan oil. Let the semolina rest a little so that it can absorb enough liquid. Meanwhile, prepare the meat. In between cooking stages, twice work cold salt water and argan oil into the *dchicha*.

Scrape the carrots and halve them lengthways. Peel the turnips and quarter; also quarter the cabbage. Cut the zucchini into sticks. Peel the pumpkin and cut into large pieces. Slice the onions thinly.

Put the dchicha on a plate. Using your fingertips, gradually work in a little hot water. Pour some argan oil into your hand and spread it through the dchicha. Once more, rub the semolina through your hands.

Fry the shank of veal briefly in the lower part of the couscous steamer. Add the onions and cover with water. Bring to the boil.

Soussia

Put the dchicha into the strainer part of the couscous steamer. Put the strainer onto the pan below, cover, and steam the dchicha for 15 minutes.

At the end of 15 minutes, season the meat with salt, pepper, ginger, and saffron. Add carrots, turnips, and a large glass of water. Steam the dchicha in 2 further stages of 15 minutes each and between the stages work in a little cold salt water and oil.

Once the vegetables are half-cooked, add zucchini, halved tomatoes, pumpkin, cabbage, parsley, and cilantro. Continue to cook the dchicha as described. Arrange in a dome on a serving platter, place the meat on top and garnish all around with pieces of vegetable.

Tagine with

Preparation time:	35 minutes
Cooking time:	1 hour 10 minutes
Difficulty:	★

Serves 4

2½ cups/400 g	*majhoul* dates
1¾ cups/200 g	shelled walnuts
	orange flower water
1⅛ lbs/500 g	shoulder of lamb
7 tbsp/100 ml	olive oil

For the marinade:

3 cloves	garlic
2	onions

1 tsp	saffron threads
1 tsp	ground ginger
1 stick	cinnamon
	salt and pepper

For the syrup:

1⅓ cups/300 g	sugar
1½ tbsp/20 ml	orange flower water
½ tsp	ground cinnamon

For the garnish:

½ cup/50 g	shelled walnuts

Among the classic dishes of Moroccan cuisine, sweet tagines are usually prepared with dried figs or apricots. If you use dates instead, this adds a touch of luxury.

This tagine is usually served at weddings. Sometimes this relatively expensive dish is served to an especially honored guest. For the Moroccans, dates are very symbolic fruits. They represent hospitality and express the respect due to the guest. If you ever have the good fortune to be a guest of a Moroccan family, you will be welcomed with milk and dates.

Khadija Bensdira, an ambassador for Moroccan culinary skill, recommends the *majhoul* variety. *Majhoul* dates, which come from the Ouarzazate region in southern Morocco, are particularly large, soft and sweet. Their

wonderful aroma goes splendidly with this tagine. To ensure that the filled dates do not collapse, move them around in the syrup very carefully.

Walnuts contain a good deal of copper and magnesium. The hard shell encloses a kernel composed of two halves, this is in turn wrapped in a dark yellowish membrane. In order to return the kernels to the condition they were in immediately after harvesting, the chef recommends soaking them for some hours in hot milk. The membrane will then come off of its own accord, and the kernels will look very appetizing.

This sophisticated tagine is a particular specialty of the royal cities. It is well suited for enjoying in the company of guests.

Stone the dates and fill them with the nuts. Soak for about 5 minutes in orange flower water.

For the marinade, place the crushed garlic cloves and chopped onions in a bowl. Add saffron threads, ginger, cinnamon sticks, salt and pepper. Pour on a glass of water and stir all the ingredients together.

Cut the shoulder of lamb into equal-sized pieces and put them in the marinade. Stir with a wooden spatula.

Walnuts and Dates

Bring the shoulder of lamb and the marinade to the boil in a saucepan, then cover with water. Bring to the boil again and then add 7 tbsp/100 ml olive oil. Cook for about 1 hour.

For the syrup, bring 3 cups/750 ml water, sugar, and orange flower water to the boil, then add cinnamon. Place the filled dates into the hot syrup. Take off the stove and put aside.

Soak the remaining nut kernels in the syrup, then dry in the oven at 300 °F/150 °C for 3–4 minutes. Arrange in the tagine, placing a further walnut kernel on each filled date.

Tagine with

Preparation time:	40 minutes
Cooking time:	45 minutes
Difficulty:	★

Serves 4

3⅓ lbs/1.5 kg	tub gurnard
2¼ lbs/1 kg	potatoes
3½ oz/100 g	red bell peppers
3½ oz/100 g	green bell peppers
2	tomatoes
2	unwaxed lemons
2 tbsp/30 ml	olive oil

For the chermoula (marinade):

1	lemon
3 cloves	garlic
1 bunch	parsley
1 bunch	cilantro (coriander)
1 tsp	paprika
1 tsp	cumin
1 stick	cinnamon
2 tbsp/30 ml	olive oil
	salt and pepper

For the garnish:

3½ oz/100 g	green olives, pits removed
½	pickled lemon

This fish tagine is a specialty of Agadir. The name of this seaside resort on Morocco's Atlantic coast can awaken feelings of sweet idleness. Thanks to its sunny climate and its miles of sandy beaches, Agadir is popular among vacationers. Agadir has a great deal to offer apart from tourist attractions: all kinds of delicious fish and seafood.

There has always been a fishing industry in Agadir, as is evident from the numerous fishing boats and canning factories. It is not surprising, therefore, that fish and seafood have a special place of honor in the regional cuisine.

Tagine with tub gurnard is a very popular dish. It is traditionally cooked over hot coals on the *kanoun*, a Moroccan clay brazier, and requires little preparation.

The tub gurnard is a relative of the ocean perch and the scorpion fish, and is not very expensive in Morocco. It is popular in fish soups, as are its relatives. Choose a fish with a firm body, tight belly, clear, protuberant eyes, shining and intact scales and red gills. Tub gurnard contains a lot of potassium and calcium and is distinguished by its lean, white, firm flesh. According to what is available in the markets, you can also use sea bream, which harmonizes just as well with *chermoula*.

Chermoula is a typical Middle Eastern blend of flavoring used in Moroccan cuisine to give numerous dishes additional taste and aroma. The marinade goes wonderfully with fish. The ingredients may vary slightly according to region and eating habits, but aromatic herbs such as flat-leaf parsley and cilantro are always included.

Cut the dorsal, belly, and tail fins off the tub gurnard. Clean and gut the fish and remove the head. Cut the fish into equal-sized slices.

For the chermoula, squeeze the juice from the lemon, crush the garlic cloves and chop the parsley as well as the cilantro. Add salt, pepper, paprika, cumin, cinnamon, and olive oil. Mix and add the pieces of tub gurnard.

Peel the potatoes and cut into slices.

Tub Gurnard

Clean the red and the green bell peppers and cut into strips. Wash the tomatoes and slice, and also the 2 lemons.

Heat the olive oil in a saucepan. Put the potatoes into the pan. Add the marinated tub gurnard. Dilute the remaining chermoula with a glass of water and pour it into the pan as well.

Add the strips of pepper and slices of lemon. Simmer on a low heat for about 30 minutes. Add the tomatoes. Continue to cook for about 15 minutes. Arrange in a tagine, and garnish with green olives and the zest of the pickled lemon.

Berber-Style

Preparation time: 30 minutes
Cooking time: 10 minutes
Difficulty: ★

Serves 4

3⅓ lbs/1.5 kg   shoulder of lamb
10½ oz/300 g   potatoes
7 oz/200 g   carrots
6 oz/180 g   zucchini
1   onion
7 oz/200 g   tomatoes

2 tbsp/30 ml   olive oil
1 stick   cinnamon
1 tsp   paprika
1 tsp   ras el-hanout (spice
                 blend)
1 bunch   cilantro (coriander)
                 salt and pepper

For the garnish:
5 oz/150g   green olives

Tagines owe their name to the glazed cone-shaped earthenware dish in which ragouts are slowly simmered. According to the family or the region from where the dishes originate, tagines can be made with lamb, poultry, or fish. The secret that contributes to the ragout's success lies in the flavorsome and very concentrated broth. It releases the flavor of the meat and intensifies the aroma of the spices.

The lamb tagine the chef is presenting here is a typical Berber dish. It is a specialty of the cities of Ouarzazate and Zagora in southern Morocco and is generally served at weddings. It is the task of the men to prepare this dish in great quantities. In the morning they bring their tagines and prepare the *kanoun* and the *brasero* on which the marinated lamb and the vegetables cook slowly for many hours. While one stirs the embers, the others join the musicians and begin to dance.

Lamb is particularly esteemed in the Berber tradition, as it is throughout the Arab world. A guest is specially honored if offered lamb. Aromatic tender shoulder of lamb is famous for its flavor.

Before setting up the tagine you must reduce the sauce as much as possible. Its flavors and aromas must develop to the full, including that of the cilantro. Cilantro is also known as "Arabian parsley," and is used in many ways in Moroccan cuisine. It is not only added to salads, soups, and sauces, but also to ragouts.

Remove the fat from the shoulder of lamb and cut into pieces.

Peel the potatoes and the carrots; rinse off the zucchini. Cut the vegetables into sticks. Peel and finely slice the onion. Wash the tomatoes and slice.

Brown the pieces of shoulder in the olive oil. Add zucchini, onion, potatoes, and carrots. Add the cinnamon stick.

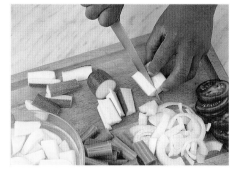

Lamb Tagine

Add the paprika and the ras el-hanout; season with salt and pepper. Add a little water and allow to cook, covered, for about 50 minutes.

Add the tomato slices and the finely chopped cilantro and cook the ragout again, covered, for 10–15 minutes.

Take out the pieces of shoulder of lamb and the vegetables. Reduce the sauce. Arrange the lamb tagine on a plate with the vegetables and sauce. Decorate with green olives.

Lamb Tagine

Preparation time: 25 minutes
Cooking time: 50 minutes
Difficulty: ★★

Serves 4

3 lbs/1.4 kg	breast of lamb
3 tbsp/45 ml	olive oil
9 oz/250 g	onions
²/₃ oz/ 20 g	garlic
½ oz/15 g	flat-leaf parsley
⅓ oz/10 g	cilantro (coriander)

1 pinch	ground ginger
1 pinch	saffron powder
2 sticks	cinnamon
	salt and pepper

For serving:

¼ cup/50 g	sugar
2 sticks	cinnamon
1 cup/150g	prunes
3 tbsp/45 ml	oil
¾ cup/100 g	blanched almonds

Moroccan gourmets have developed an endless variety of different *tajines rghalmi*, lamb tagines. As this dish by Mohammed Aïtali combines the aroma of tender meat with soft poached prunes and the crunchy fried almonds, it bears the sonorous Arabic name of *tajine barkouk bel louz*. According to taste, *tajine rghalmi* is sometimes prepared with a selection of different vegetables (green beans, carrots, zucchini, and turnips), with onions and raisins, with almonds alone, with sugared quinces, pears, dried apricots, or with a mixture of olives and pickled lemons.

The foundation of this dish is breast of lamb, including some of the flank and shoulder. Among Moroccan cooks, shoulder of lamb is considered a meat that can be used to do practically anything in a wide range of differing dishes. There is even an Arabic proverb advising inexperienced cooks: "If you know nothing about cooking, ask the butcher for a piece of shoulder."

The most common type of sheep in Morocco is known as *sardi*. The animals have a fairly long body, are correspondingly heavy and have a white fleece with black patches. They are bred in the plain of Casablanca, better know for cereal production, and in the Meknès region, and in the central Atlas Mountains in the vicinity of Beni Melal. *Sardi* are particularly prized during *Aïd el-kebir* when Moroccan families prepare mutton in all imaginable versions.

The chef poaches the prunes in a syrup scented with cinnamon. If you wish to make the flavor even more intense, add slices of lemon, ground pepper, and orange flower water. Prunes also go excellently with tagines of beef or lamb.

Bone the breast of lamb. Cut the meat into equal-sized cubes of about 2 oz/50 g.

Heat the olive oil in a pan. When hot, put the pieces of meat in and brown on all sides.

Peel and chop onions and garlic. Also chop the parsley and cilantro. Add all these to the meat. Sprinkle with ginger, salt, pepper, and saffron. Add sticks of cinnamon.

with Prunes

Pour on enough cold water to cover all the ingredients. Simmer, covered, for about 30 minutes, until the meat is good and tender.

Put sugar and sticks of cinnamon into a pot with water. Add prunes and poach for about 10 minutes on medium heat.

Heat the oil in another pot. Put the almonds into the hot oil and allow them to turn golden brown. Place the meat in the center of a serving platter. Garnish with prunes, fried almonds, and parsley.

Atlas-Style

Preparation time: 45 minutes
Cooking time: 1 hour 5 minutes
Difficulty: ★★

Serves 4

8	quails
2 cloves	garlic
2	onions
1 bunch	parsley
1 bunch	cilantro (coriander)
4 tbsp/60 ml	olive oil
4 tbsp/60 ml	peanut oil

1 pinch	ginger
2 pinches	saffron threads
2 pinches	Moroccan saffron powder for coloring
²/₃ cup/150 ml	chicken stock
1 ¹/₃ lbs/600 g	fresh spinach
12	quail's eggs
¹/₂ stick/50 g	fresh (unsalted) butter
	salt and pepper

Quail tagines are among the most sophisticated delicacies that Moroccan cuisine has to offer. Bouchaïb Kama is never short of good ideas, and here introduces us to one of his most recent creations; small pieces of quail with delicious balls of spinach and quail's eggs glazed with saffron and butter, in a sauce of saffron and onions.

The tagine owes its name to a container made of glazed earthenware with a cone-shaped lid used for cooking. The Moroccans have retained the custom of cooking over a *majmar*, a ceramic container filled with hot coals. It is difficult to find the handsome tagine pots outside Morocco. If you do not have one, the chef recommends that you at least serve the dish in another earthenware vessel with a colorful border.

The quails used by the chef come from the Atlas Mountains, where there are several farms rearing quails. Quails shot in the wild are not on offer in Moroccan restaurants, as their origin is too uncertain and they are often too full of shotgun pellets. Quails shot by family members are eaten within the family only. Quail farms make it possible for these birds to be available all the year round. For this recipe you can, however, also use turkey, chicken, rabbit, or duck.

The small, rather expensive quail's eggs with their little brown spots are often used to garnish very sophisticated dishes, such as those served at receptions. In provincial parts of Morocco old people still maintain that hard-boiled quail's eggs eaten in the morning help to cure asthma.

Clean and gut the quails and rinse them under running water. Cut off the necks, wingtips and thighs. Carve the bodies lengthways and cut into 2 parts, giving 6 pieces per quail.

Peel the garlic and the onions and chop. Also chop the parsley and cilantro. Fry the quails in both kinds of oil. Season with salt and pepper. Add garlic, onions, ginger, 2 pinches of saffron threads and saffron powder. Fry until the quails are browned.

When the quails have simmered for about 10 minutes on a medium heat, add the chicken stock and stir.

Quail Tagine

Add the parsley and cilantro at once. Cover. Cook for a further 25–30 minutes.

Scald the spinach in salt water. Pour on cold water to keep the green color. Press out the liquid and chop finely. Roll into small balls with your hands.

Boil the quail's eggs for 5 minutes and then shell them. Melt the butter in a small pan. Stir in 1 pinch of saffron powder. Put in the quail's eggs and move them around in the saffron butter until they are yellow all over. Arrange the dish on a serving platter.

Conger Eel

Preparation time:	45 minutes
Soaking time:	15 minutes
Marinating time:	10 minutes
Cooking time:	45 minutes
Difficulty:	☆

Serves 8

3 cups/500 g	raisins
4½ lbs/2 kg	conger eel
2¼ lbs/1 kg	onions
4 tbsp/60 ml	oil
2 sticks	cinnamon

For the chermoula sauce:

1 bunch	parsley
1 bunch	cilantro (coriander)
1 pinch	ground cinnamon
1 pinch	Moroccan saffron powder for coloring
4 tbsp	oil
	salt and pepper

For serving (as desired):

2 or 3	fresh unwaxed lemons

Tagines are an essential part of Moroccan cuisine. Not only meat and poultry, but conger eels, dorades, sea bream, croakers, and sea bass are prepared in this manner. This eel tagine is typical of the southern regions, especially of the area around Agadir, the famous coastal resort, the home town of the chef.

Agadir and Safi are the two most important harbor cities in Morocco. Here there is an excess of eel. The daily catch is so great that numerous factories canning the fish or processing it in other ways have been set up right by the quays. There are also great quantities of other kinds of fish, such as sardines, sea bream, and red mullet.

Conger eels prefer living in the open sea, such as the deep waters of the Gulf of Agadir. In general, the chef uses eels weighing three to four pounds (1½–2 kg), but some can exceed ten pounds (4½ kg). A medium-sized eel, paradoxically, provides more meat than a large one because the spine of a large one is much thicker and there is more waste. Eels are difficult to fillet, so they are always cooked in thick slices with the skin and spine left on. This also helps to ensure that the meat does not fall apart during cooking.

This recipe is usually cooked in the tagine in which the dish is then served. All the guests help themselves from the common dish and fill their plates as they wish. Finally large pieces of Moroccan bread are used to sop up the delicious sauce left on the plates and dishes. Abdelmalek al-Meraoui serves the dish to guests in his restaurant in small tagine dishes.

Soak the raisins for 15 minutes in a bowl of warm water. Remove the head of the eel. Cut the fish into large chunks and cut these into slices about ¾ inch/1.5 cm thick. Do not remove the skin.

Chop the parsley and cilantro. Peel the onions and slice thinly.

In a large bowl, combine parsley, cilantro, cinnamon, salt, pepper, saffron powder, and oil to make a chermoula. Turn the slices of eel in the chermoula. Marinate for 10 minutes.

Tagine

Place the slices of onion in an oven-proof dish. Distribute the drained raisins over these. Sprinkle with oil and dust with a little cinnamon. Brown in the oven for 15 minutes.

Cover the bottom of a tagine dish with the onions and raisins. Place the cinnamon sticks on top.

Place the marinated slices of eel on the bed of onions. In a bowl, mix the remaining chermoula with a little water and pour over the eel and the onions. Cover and cook for 30 minutes. Serve hot, with wedges of lemon.

Shrimp

Preparation time: 30 minutes
Cooking time: 25 minutes
Difficulty: ★

Serves 4

2 cups/400 g	Basmati rice
½ stick/50 g	butter
24 medium	shrimp
1 large	onion
2 cloves	garlic
1 bunch	flat-leaf parsley

1 bunch	cilantro (coriander)
4 medium	fresh tomatoes
1 tbsp/15 ml	olive oil
1 tbsp/15 ml	peanut oil
¼ tsp/1 g	saffron threads
½ envelope	Moroccan saffron powder for coloring
1 tsp	sweet pimento powder
2 tbsp	tomato paste
1 or 2	fresh unwaxed lemons
	salt and pepper

The shrimp tagine is one of the most frequently cooked recipes in Morocco. Thanks to excellent transport facilities, dishes using fish and seafood have long since reached the interior of the country.

Morocco's coast is 2,175 miles (3,500 kilometers) long, and is unequally divided between the Atlantic and the Mediterranean. In these waters there are more than 7,000 types of marine life, of which 65 percent are fishes, crustaceans, and mollusks. The most important fishing grounds for shrimp are along the northern Atlantic coast between Tan Tan and Tangier. Fishing for shrimp takes place all year round.

For his tagine, Bouchaïb Kama has chosen medium-sized common shrimp. He counts on six shrimp per person. For a more sophisticated presentation, he leaves the tails on. You can, however, remove the whole shell.

As an accompaniment, Bouchaïb Kama serves Basmati rice, which is characterized by longish grains and an aromatic flavor. However, it needs constant monitoring while cooking, as it softens more quickly than other types of rice. You will find that the grains extend lengthways while cooking and become soft very quickly. The chef mixes the cooked rice with butter, covers it with aluminum foil and keeps it warm in the oven or on the burner. The rice then continues to absorb moisture and swells a little more until the shrimp tagine is done.

The sauce will thicken, even without flour or starch, because of the tomato paste, the fresh tomatoes, and the olive oil. Do not mix in the chopped cilantro and parsley until shortly before serving. This is the best way for the sauce to absorb the aroma of the herbs.

Bring salt water to the boil in a pot. Put the rice in the boiling water and cook for 8–10 minutes. Add a piece of butter, cover and keep warm.

Remove the heads of the shrimp. Carefully remove the shells with the tips of your fingers. Leave the tails if desired.

Peel the onion and garlic. Chop finely. Also chop the parsley and cilantro. Remove stalks from the tomatoes and rinse.

Tagine

Heat a second pot of water. Put the tomatoes into the hot water. As soon as the skins begin to peel off, take the tomatoes out of the water with a slotted spatula. Put them into a bowl of iced water and remove the skins.

On a high heat, heat up the olive and peanut oil mixture with the onions, garlic, saffron threads, and powder, pimento, salt and pepper. Add the shrimp and fry briefly. Then add the tomato paste, mixed with water, and fresh tomatoes. Cook for another 5 minutes.

Add parsley and cilantro. Leave the pot on the burner for another few moments and stir until the sauce thickens slightly. Serve with wedges of lemon.

King Shrimp

Preparation time:	35 minutes
Cooking time:	20 minutes
Difficulty:	☆

Serves 4

8	king shrimp
1¾ lbs/800 g	potatoes
2	onions
4 cloves	garlic
1 bunch	cilantro (coriander)

1 bunch	parsley
1 pinch	saffron threads
3 tbsp/45 ml	olive oil
4	tomatoes
	salt and pepper

For the garnish:

1 leaf	parsley
1	pickled lemon
10½ oz/300 g	pickled black olives

This tagine with king shrimp is the special creation of the chef. It is not difficult to make and is reminiscent of the tempting aromas and colors of the Mediterranean countries.

King shrimp are sizeable and can be easily recognized by their bright red color. Their delicious flesh needs only a little time to cook. They can be found everywhere in Moroccan markets, but they can also be replaced by North Sea shrimp. Monkfish or dorade are also suitable for this tagine.

In this dish, new potatoes combine marvelously with the shrimp. Potatoes are originally from South America and today are eaten all over the world. Potatoes are cultivated all over North Africa and in the spring Moroccan new potatoes are exported to Europe. Choose potatoes with a smooth skin and no visible eyes or blemishes. Keep them in a cool, dry place that is as dark as possible.

This very aromatic tagine benefits particularly from the aroma of parsley. The parsley should be a deep green and fresh, and also have firm stalks and leaves.

The chef salts the garlic a little to make its powerful aroma a little milder. Garlic originated in Central Asia and has been cultivated for over 5,000 years. It is considered good for the circulation and is much esteemed all over the Mediterranean and used for many savory dishes. The cloves should be firm and plump.

If you want to emphasize the aromas of this dish further, the chef recommends adding a little lemon juice shortly before the start of the cooking time.

Shell the shrimp but do not remove the heads.

Peel the potatoes and cut into large cubes. Place in a bowl of water and put aside.

Peel the onions and garlic and chop them. Rinse cilantro and parsley and chop them as well. Fry lightly in a pan with the saffron threads in the olive oil. Season with salt and pepper.

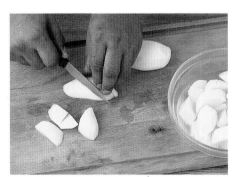

Tagine

Scald and skin the tomatoes. Then remove the seeds and dice them finely. Cut the olives and the lemon for the garnish into small pieces. Put aside.

Put the drained potatoes into the pan with the onions. Stir. Add a glass of water. Cook for about 10 minutes.

Add the shrimp. Cook for about 6 minutes. Add the cubes of tomato. Allow to simmer for a few moments. Arrange the shrimp tagine on a serving plate and pour over the sauce. Garnish with the pieces of olive and lemon and a leaf of parsley.

Tagine with

Preparation time: 40 minutes
Cooking time: 30 minutes
Difficulty: ★★

Serves 4–6

3⅓ lbs/1.5 kg   monkfish
9 oz/250 g   purple olives
1   lemon

For the chermoula sauce:
2 cloves   garlic
1 bunch   cilantro (coriander)

1 bunch   parsley
2 oz/50 g   pickled lemon
2 pinches   paprika
2 pinches   cumin
1 pinch   ground ginger
2   fresh lemons
1 tbsp   argan oil
                 salt and pepper

Monkfish, served on festive occasions only, is caught in Morocco both in Mediterranean and Atlantic coastal waters. The industrial deep-sea fishing trawlers bring only small quantities to land. In contrast to their European colleagues, Moroccan fishermen sell monkfish with the head, which is disproportionately large. You can sometimes find fish without the head or even fillets cut directly on the fishing boat.

Monkfish have a sturdy spine, which is not hard to remove. Each fish contains two large fillets, which can easily be cut into medallions. Even after a longer cooking period, the white flesh remains firm and attractive. For this reason, Moroccan cooks like to use monkfish for couscous, tagines with tomatoes and onions, or with chopped tomatoes, lemons, potatoes, and red olives.

The monkfish tagine has a unique aroma typical of the south-west of Morocco. This special touch is due to the argan oil that comes from the fruits of the argan trees, which grow in large numbers between Essaouira and Agadir. This oil is mentioned as early as the 13th century by the first Arab geographers. After watching goats climb into the argan trees to eat the fruit, the traveler Ali Ibn Baytar is said to have spread the rumor, still current today, that the oil was extracted from goat droppings.

Black or purple olives can be added to the sauce at the end of the cooking process. These fruits are fully ripe, after going first through a green, then a red, and finally a purple stage. The small picholine olives, known as *beldi* in Morocco, are pickled in brine, as are the *Ascolana dura*, *Ascolana tenera*, and *Meslala*.

Carve the monkfish. Remove the 2 fillets from the spine, one after the other. Cut into medallions.

For the chermoula, chop the garlic, cilantro, parsley, and pickled lemon. Sweat half the cilantro, parsley, and garlic, salt, pepper, 1 pinch each of paprika, and cumin, ginger and the juice of 1 lemon in the oil, then add the pickled lemon.

Season the chermoula with saffron threads. Stir and put aside.

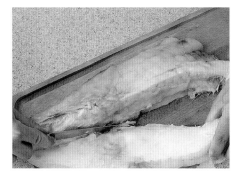

Monkfish and Argan Oil

For the chermoula marinade, mix the remaining cilantro and parsley and the remaining garlic thoroughly with 1 pinch each of paprika and cumin, salt and the juice of 1 lemon. Add the medallions of monkfish and coat with the marinade.

Put the marinated monkfish medallions into the pan with the chermoula prepared previously. Cook, covered, for about 20 minutes.

Heat water with a little lemon juice in a small saucepan. Poach the olives in this liquid. Drain and fry for a moment in the, by now, reduced chermoula. Serve immediately.

Chicken

Preparation time: 30 minutes
Cooking time: 55 minutes
Difficulty: ★★

Serves 8

2 small	chickens
1 clove	garlic
9 oz/250 g	onions
1 bunch	parsley
1 bunch	cilantro (coriander)

7 tbsp/100 ml	olive oil
1 pinch	ground ginger
1 pinch	saffron powder
3 or 4	cinnamon sticks
1 pinch	saffron threads
1	lemon
4	eggs
	a little white vinegar
	salt and pepper

This dish is best served in a decorative tagine vessel, placed in the center of the table with its delicious contents drawing the expectant glances of the guests. This tagine is a specialty from the town of Souira, a coastal resort not far from Agadir. The mixture of eggs and parsley, poured over the chicken cooked in a brown sauce, gives a distinct and original touch to the dish. After adding the egg mixture, the lid of the pot is closed and the dish is cooked for another ten minutes until the eggs are set.

Like many of his countrymen, the chef first cleans the chickens thoroughly with salt and vinegar and then rinses them off under running water before preparing them. In this way, the meat is once again cleansed of possible impurities according to religious rules.

In general, the Moroccan *beldi* chicken, reared by farmers, has a red, firm flesh. It needs somewhat longer to cook than mass-produced chicken.

In our recipe, the chicken is completely boned and then cut into pieces. The fillets and the thigh meat are cooked in the sauce in the tagine dish. Depending on your kitchen equipment, various cooking methods are possible. The chef has allowed the chicken to simmer in a casserole for a long time and then puts it into the tagine dish with the mixture to finish cooking. Many Moroccan cooks, however, prefer to carry out the whole cooking process in the tagine dish in which the meal is later served. If you don't have a tagine, it can also be perfectly cooked in a simple pan or an oven-proof casserole dish.

Rub the chickens with vinegar and salt to clean them, then rinse. Carve on the belly side on both sides of the breastbone and follow the breastbone with the knife to remove breast fillets and thighs. Cut the meat into smaller pieces.

Peel and chop the garlic and onions, and also chop the parsley and cilantro.

Heat the olive oil in a heavy pan. Add the onions to the hot oil, sweat and then add the pieces of chicken.

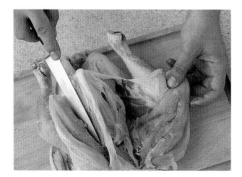

Mkaddam Souiri

Sprinkle the pieces of chicken with cilantro, three-quarters of the parsley, salt, pepper, and garlic.

Add ginger, saffron powder, saffron threads, cinnamon sticks, and lemon juice to the pieces of chicken and stir. Cook for 40 minutes, covered.

Break the eggs into a bowl. Mix in the remaining parsley. Put the chicken pieces into the tagine dish and pour the egg mixture over them. Cover and cook for a further 10 minutes. Serve hot in the tagine dish.

Chicken

Preparation time: 25 minutes
Soaking time: 15 minutes
Cooking time: 1 hour and 15 minutes
Difficulty: ★★

Serves 4

1	chicken, 3⅓ lbs/1.5 kg
3½ oz/100 g	coarse salt
3½ oz/100 g	chicken stomachs
3½ oz/100 g	chicken livers
7 tbsp/100 ml	white vinegar
12½ oz/350 g	onions
4 tbsp/60 ml	olive oil
2	pickled lemons
9 oz/250 g	red olives

For the chermoula sauce:

1 bunch	fresh cilantro (coriander)
½ tsp/2 g	saffron threads
1 envelope	Moroccan saffron powder for coloring
1 tsp/5 g	ground cumin
1 tsp/5 g	ground cinnamon
1 tsp/5 g	ginger
1 oz/30 g	garlic
	salt
1	lemon

M'quali is one of the most widespread and popular recipes in Morocco. The chicken is simmered in a yellow sauce with saffron and ginger and finally garnished with red olives and pickled lemons. Amina Khayar, always at pains to impart flavor and sophistication to her dishes, loosens the skin of the chicken and introduces a paste of herbs, spices, and lemons between the skin and the meat.

Apart from *m'quali*, in Moroccan cuisine there are another three sauces that are regularly used in ragouts and tagines: *qadra*, a yellow purée of onions flavored with saffron, *smen* (preserved butter), and pepper; red *m'hammar*, spiced with paprika, cumin, and olive oil; and *m'chermel* with plenty of cilantro and parsley.

In order to meet the demands of Islamic rules on food preparation, the chef immerses the chicken and the giblets

in water mixed with vinegar, thus removing traces of blood, impurities, and excess fat. She then rinses the chicken thoroughly under running water. According to preference, you can cook the chicken giblets in the sauce for the chicken or mix them into the marinade and the pitted olives making up the flavoring paste.

Some prefer *m'quali* chicken with a light sauce with added water. Others reduce the sauce as far as possible until the oil rises to the surface. At weddings, *m'quali* chickens are often served in a very creamy sauce, with three being served on a pretty *Taou* faience plate from Fez.

Once the chicken is cooked, it is served with olives and pickled lemons. You can also take it out of the sauce and fry it crisp and brown in oil. When eating, everyone mops up the sauce with Moroccan bread.

Cut off the wingtips of the chicken and remove excess fat. Loosen the skin from the flesh by sliding your hand underneath, but without removing the skin.

Distribute a handful of coarse salt between the flesh and the skin of the chicken. Also salt the chicken stomachs and livers. Soak the chicken for 15 minutes in water mixed with vinegar. Rinse under running water, drain, and pat dry.

For the chermoula, mix cilantro, saffron threads, saffron powder, cumin, cinnamon, ginger, crushed garlic, salt, lemon juice, and a little water. Place the chicken in the mixture and carefully rub the chermoula over the flesh.

M'quali

Brown the chicken in a casserole, turning regularly and repeatedly pouring water over it.

Add chopped onions, chopped giblets, a good splash of olive oil, and water. Cook, covered, for 45 minutes.

Add the chicken livers to the pot and cook for a further 10 minutes. At the end of the cooking time, add olives and pickled lemon.

Fish & Seafood

Grilled Essaouira

Preparation time: 35 minutes
Marinating time: 2 hours
Cooking time: 20 minutes
Difficulty: ★

Serves 4

1⅓ lbs/600 g	swordfish
2	green bell peppers
2	red bell peppers
½ stick/50 g	butter
1 cup/200 g	rice
1 tsp	paprika powder
1 tbsp/15 ml	vegetable oil
	salt

For the marinade:

6 cloves	garlic
1 bunch	parsley
1 bunch	cilantro (coriander)
1 tsp	chile powder
½ tsp	cumin
1 tsp	paprika powder
1	lemon
	salt and pepper

Essaouira, which is well protected by its red and ochre fortifications, is determined to preserve its grand houses with their blue shutters. This charming Phoenician town with its square grid of streets is well known for its maritime life.

You should go to the harbor of an evening to watch the fishing boats tie up. The quays, which seemed quite sleepy beforehand, suddenly come to life. Many people gather there, attracted by the cries of the market-stall holders advertising their wares. Business is at its height at the fish stalls wedged in between the colorful boats and trawlers. Tempting odors of broiled skewers of fish arise from the *kanouns* and *braseros*. Essaouira is full of life.

The people of Essaouira love everything the sea offers them as food, and miss no opportunity of enjoying it. The

swordfish skewers are sometimes grilled directly by the shore. They are very popular and also suitable for a meal with guests. At the same time, they are easy to make.

Swordfish live in great numbers in warm ocean waters and are impressively big. They are very popular as they have excellent, tender flesh, but tuna is just as suitable for this recipe. Generally, swordfish are sold in cut pieces. The tail and the fins are also edible.

Grilling the skewers over hot coals is one of the oldest methods of cooking this fish. Some people add a little lamb fat to give the fish additional aroma. Wait until all the charcoal is glowing before you start grilling the fish.

For the marinade, put the crushed garlic cloves, chopped parsley, chopped coriander, chile powder, cumin, and paprika into a salad bowl. Squeeze the lemon and add the juice. Season with salt and pepper and mix together all the ingredients.

Cut the swordfish into strips and then into regular cubes. Place these in the marinade and stir carefully. Marinate for at least 2 hours.

Wash the green and red bell peppers and remove seeds. Cut into very small cubes.

Fish Skewers

Melt the butter in a pan. Add the rice and the cubes of pepper. Sweat for about 3 minutes.

Add 1 tsp of paprika powder and season with salt. Cover with water and cook, covered, for 12–15 minutes.

Take the swordfish cubes out of the marinade and put onto skewers. Drizzle with oil. Cook on the grill and then arrange on plates with some of the rice.

Tangier-Style

Preparation time: 30 minutes
Cooking time: 30 minutes
Difficulty: ★★

Serves 4

2¼ lbs/1 kg	calamaries (small squid)
1¼ cups/250 g	rice
1 bunch	flat-leaf parsley
1 bunch	cilantro (coriander)

3½ oz/100 g	garlic
4 tbsp/60ml	olive oil
2 pinches	cayenne pepper
	salt and pepper

For the garnish:

| 1 | green lemon |

The calamaries introduced here by M'hamed Chahid are filled with a mixture of garlic, herbs, and rice and served in a savory red sauce. In his restaurant, the chef often serves them on a bed of parsley and pours sauce over them.

All year round, Moroccan fishermen supply the country with numerous mollusks such as calamaries, octopus, and squid. They are all available in the markets: the smallest are known as *chipirons, puntia,* or *supions.* For this traditional dish, the chef uses medium-sized calamaries seven to eight inches in length. It is possible to find large specimens up to two feet in length.

The Moroccans particularly prize calamaries with a filling of whiting and *chermoula.* The little harbor restaurants also offer these broiled to passers-by.

After removing the head, you should also take out the beak-like jaws in the center of the tentacles. To do this, open the ring of tentacles, press on the head with two fingers so that the "beak" comes into view, and then firmly draw it out.

The rice is first cooked in boiling water, but it should be taken off the heat once it is soft but not quite cooked through. It will then continue to swell inside the calamaries while these simmer in the sauce.

The chef recommends serving this dish with green lemon; its taste refines the strong aroma of the calamaries. In the old quarters of many Moroccan cities there are still houses with courtyards where lemon trees grow. All those living in the house can help themselves as they wish.

To clean the calamaries, hold the head and carefully draw out the innards. Remove the bone. Thoroughly rinse the mantle. Cut off the tentacles and remove the "beak." Blanch the tentacles for 5 minutes in boiling water. Put the mantles aside.

Bring salted water to the boil in a pot. Add the rice and cook for 10 minutes.

Chop the parsley, cilantro, and poached tentacles, one after the other. Peel the garlic and chop finely.

Stuffed Calamaries

Pour a little olive oil into a pot. Add the rice, three-quarters of the cilantro and the parsley, 3 oz/80 g of garlic and the tentacles. Stir while on the heat.

Season the rice filling with pepper, salt, and 1 pinch of cayenne pepper. Fry for 3–4 minutes, stirring.

Fill the mantles with the rice mixture. Close the opening with a toothpick. Fry the calamaries in olive oil with the cilantro, parsley, and garlic that has been kept aside and add salt, pepper, and 1 pinch of cayenne pepper. Cook for 10 minutes in the sauce. Serve.

"Old Harbor"

Preparation time: 30 minutes
Cooking time: 25 minutes
Difficulty: ★★

Serves 4

1⅛ lbs/500 g	sea bass
10½ oz/300 g	small calamaries (small squid)
3½ oz/100 g	button mushrooms
4½ oz/125 g	shrimp, ready to cook
¼ stick/30 g	unsalted butter
7 oz/200 g	Chinese rice noodles
12½ oz/350 g	*yufka* pastry dough sheets
1	egg
	oil

For the marinade:

⅓ oz/10 g	flat-leaf parsley
⅔ oz/20 g	fresh cilantro (coriander)
1 pinch	paprika
1 pinch	ground cumin
⅓ oz/10 g	garlic
1 oz/30 g	pickled lemon
5⅕ tbsp/80 ml	olive oil
	salt and pepper

For the garnish:

⅔ oz/20 g	flat-leaf parsley
4	fresh lemons
4	medium king shrimp

The Oudaïa casbah, built in the 12th century, served in the 17th century as a refuge for pirates. Today, at the ends of the narrow ancient streets, boats from Rabat daily unload sardines, sea bass, or red mullet onto the quays of the Bou Regreg. In the capital, only small boats can easily pass the "barrier" separating the Bou Regreg from the Atlantic. On the ocean, the boats never go far from the coast to fish.

Alongside sole and sea bream, the sea bass, which the chef uses for this *pastilla* (pastry), is one of the most popular fish in Morocco. Moroccan cooks distinguish between the dark-backed sea bass caught in the Atlantic and the spotted variety that occurs only in the Mediterranean.

Calamaries can be found in the markets in Morocco all year round. They come in different sizes; the largest are very pale and can reach a length of up to two feet. However, you should choose smaller specimens for this pastry.

The chef stir-fries the ingredients for the filling in a pan. If, however, you are preparing large quantities, it would be better to place the ingredients in an ovenproof dish and pre-cook them in the oven.

The hand-made sheets of pastry dough are very fine and thin. Plenty of patience is needed to separate them without tearing. Spread a whole sheet of pastry out on the work surface and place a piece of another sheet in the center to avoid the filling leaking out. Put a little filling on this second piece, wrap the pastry to form a rectangular "parcel" and then fold it into a second sheet. All you need to do now is fry it in the pan.

Starting at the gills, carve the sea bass. Run the knife along the backbone to remove the 2 fillets. Skin the fillets. Cut the flesh into small cubes.

Clean and gut the calamaries and also cut these into small cubes. Cut off the bottom part of the stalk of the button mushrooms, then rinse, peel, and slice thinly.

For the marinade: mix chopped parsley, chopped cilantro, paprika, cumin, crushed garlic, chopped pickled lemon, salt, pepper, and olive oil. Add cubes of calamaries, shelled shrimp, and pieces of fish. Place all ingredients in a pan with the melted butter.

Pastry

Add the button mushrooms and fry for a few moments. Pour on a little cold water. Cook on a high heat, stirring. In another pan, cook the rice noodles in boiling water until soft, drain, put into the pan and cook for 5 minutes with the other ingredients.

Place the cooled filling on a sheet of yufka pastry dough. Fold into a rectangle, place on a second sheet of dough and once again fold all the edges over the middle to make a rectangle. Stick down the "seams" with beaten egg.

Fry the pastries in hot oil until golden brown on both sides, turning carefully from time to time with a spatula. Garnish with parsley, lemon, and king shrimp, and serve warm.

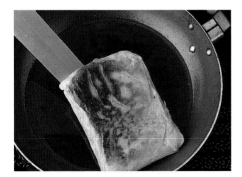

Monkfish with

Preparation time:	35 minutes
Cooking time:	30 minutes
Difficulty:	★

Serves 4

1⅛ lbs/500 g	tomatoes
1	onion
1 tbsp/15 ml	argan oil
½ tsp/2 g	ground cinnamon
2 tbsp/30 g	sugar
1⅓ lbs/600 g	monkfish fillets
10 stems	rosemary
6½ tbsp/100 g	butter

2	eggs
1⅛ lbs/500 g	sheets of *yufka* pastry dough
	salt and pepper

For the vinaigrette:

2	unwaxed lemons
2 tbsp	argan oil
1	tomato
	salt and pepper

For the garnish (as desired):

Moroccan saffron powder for coloring

Monkfish with tomato sauce is a creation of the chef Lahoussine Bel Moufid. As chef at the Sheraton in Casablanca, he is a master of the finer points of Moroccan cuisine. Despite his training in Canada and the United States, he is passionately devoted to the traditions of his forefathers, and based on these foundations he creates original and very tasty dishes.

For this recipe, he has been inspired by a typical Moroccan dessert by the name of *resda*, which is based on almonds. This spiral-shaped pastry owes its name to the turban the men wear bound around their heads. For this recipe, however, Lahoussine Bel Moufid has replaced the almonds with sweet-savory cooked tomatoes.

The tomato sauce is the perfect accompaniment to monkfish, known for its juicy flesh reminiscent of lobster.

Each medallion of monkfish is stuck onto a stem of rosemary and then cooked on a grill. Rosemary is a small, evergreen shrub that is native to the Mediterranean region. Its leaves are very fragrant, and are used fresh or dried, as a flavoring.

A lover of the produce of his home country, the chef crowns his creation with a vinaigrette made from argan oil. This has been produced from the fruits of the argan tree, which grows only in the Essaouira region, for thousands of years. It is not only a culinary delicacy, but is known for its pharmaceutical and cosmetic effectiveness. As early as 1219, the Egyptian physician Ibn Baytar praised the powers of the oil tree in his writings. The oil is cold-pressed and produced by hand by the Berber women. Over 60 pounds (30 kilos) of fruit are needed for a quart (1 liter) of oil—and it takes 15 hours to produce this quantity!

Blanch all the tomatoes in salt water, including those for the vinaigrette. Dice finely and put 4 tbsp aside for the vinaigrette. Peel and chop the onion.

Sweat the onion in 1 tbsp of argan oil. Add the diced tomatoes and cook for about 10 minutes.

Add cinnamon and sugar. For the vinaigrette, squeeze 1 lemon and dice the other. Put the juice into a bowl, add argan oil, salt, pepper, diced lemon, and the reserved diced tomato. Mix.

Tomato Sauce

Cut the fillets of monkfish into medallions. Cut the rosemary stems to size. Thread each medallion onto a rosemary stem. Broil.

Melt the butter. Separate the eggs, put the yolks into a bowl and beat. Spread out the sheets of pastry dough and brush with melted butter. Put a little of the tomato sauce on each. Keep some sauce to garnish.

Roll up pastry sheets like a cigar. Stick down the edges with egg yolk and roll into a spiral shape. Bake for 10 minutes at 350 °F/180 °C. Serve with tomato sauce, medallions of monkfish, the vinaigrette, and a little saffron.

Sea Bass with

Preparation time: 30 minutes
Marinating time: 15 minutes
Cooking time: 25 minutes
Difficulty: ★★

Serves 4

4	sea bass, each about 12 oz/350 g
4 cloves	garlic
1¼ lb/560 g	onions
1 bunch	parsley
1 bunch	cilantro (coriander)
	salt and pepper

2	lemons
1¾ cups/320 g	large *majhoul* dates
1⅔ cups/200 g	shelled walnuts
4 tbsp/60 ml	olive oil
4 tbsp/60 ml	peanut oil
½ envelope	saffron threads
½ envelope	Moroccan saffron powder for coloring

For the garnish:

2	lemons
4	medium tomatoes

Several chefs have taken part in creating this dish. In keeping with tradition, they have combined sweet flavors with savory, but have developed the traditional recipe a stage further. The result is a combination of marinated sea bass with a mixture of herbs and spices and the sweet dates filled with walnuts.

There are two types of sea bass living in Moroccan waters: one with a dark back, and a spotted one that is especially widespread in the Mediterranean. With its fine white flesh, the fish is used for many delicacies in Morocco: skewers, fillets, rolled in beaten egg with herbs and spices (parsley, cumin, cilantro, salt, and pepper) and fried, or in tagines with fresh vegetables (potatoes, olives, pickled lemons).

In Morocco, guests are offered dates and milk as an expression of hospitality. The chef recommends *majhoul*

dates for this dish, as they are large, fleshy, and very sweet. Morocco is not so well known as Tunisia as a producer of dates, yet innumerable different varieties of dates ripen here: the relatively small and pale *boussekri* or the somewhat yellowish *bleuh* are only two examples.

Far south, there are almost a million date palms in the luscious green, water-rich oases of the Tafilalet. Their fruit is harvested at the end of September. In early October, the date festival is held in Erfoud. For three days, Berber tribes, hoteliers, dealers, and tourists all celebrate this small desert fruit.

In his restaurant, Bouchaïb Kama drizzles a sauce of onions and saffron over the sea bass. In this version, he has distributed the sauce around the fish to show off the fish and dates to better effect.

Cut off the fins and the tip of the tail from the sea bass with fish scissors. Cut into the fish at the gills and a little on the belly. Clean and gut, and rinse under running water.

Chop the garlic, onions (put 10 oz/280 g of these aside afterwards), parsley and cilantro. Mix with salt, pepper, and lemon juice. Stuff the fish with this mixture and allow to soak in for 15 minutes.

Open the dates carefully along one side (without cutting them in two) and remove the pits. Fill each date with a walnut kernel.

Majhoul Dates

Heat both types of oil in a deep pan. Add the reserved onions and fry briefly. Add saffron threads and saffron powder. Sweat the onions, stirring, on a low heat.

Place the stuffed sea bass on this bed of onions and saffron.

Arrange the filled dates around the fish. Add the remaining marinade and a little water. Cover the pan with a piece of aluminum foil and place in the oven for 15 minutes. Reduce the sauce a little and then beat with butter. Garnish, if you wish.

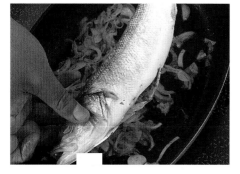
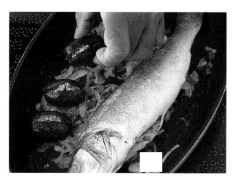

Stuffed

Preparation time:	1 hour 10 minutes
Marinating time:	2 hours
Cooking time:	40 minutes
Difficulty:	★★

Serves 4

1	sea bass, weighing approximately 4¹/₂ lbs/2 kg
2	lemons
2¹/₄ lbs/1 kg	tomatoes
1¹/₈ lb/500 g	green, red, and yellow bell peppers
7 oz/200 g	onions
7 tbsp/100 ml	olive oil

For the chermoula sauce:

6 cloves	garlic
1 bunch	parsley
1 bunch	cilantro (coriander)
1 pinch	chile powder
1 tsp	paprika
¹/₂ tsp	cumin
7 tbsp/100 ml	white vinegar
1 tsp	tomato paste
	salt and pepper

For the filling:

1 cup/200 g	rice
4 tbsp	tomato paste
7 oz/200 g	shelled shrimp
3¹/₂ oz/100 g	pickled lemons
2 oz/50 g	purple olives, pitted

For the garnish:

2 oz/50 g	shelled shrimp

This stuffed sea bass is a delicacy, usually served only at major festivals. It is a specialty of the royal city of Fez.

Sea bass are plentiful in the Mediterranean. The fish is highly prized for its firm, lean, and delicious flesh. It can be poached, flambéed, fried or stuffed. Keep an eye on it while cooking, as the flesh can fall apart rapidly. When fresh, its body is firm, smelling slightly of iodine, its scales gleam, the eyes protrude slightly, and its gills are pink. Depending on what is available in the market, you can also replace it with common pandora, dorade, or sea bream.

In this recipe the fish is flavored with *chermoula*. The mixture of garlic, parsley, cilantro, paprika, cumin, tomato paste, chile powder, salt, pepper, and white vinegar not only acts as a flavoring but also makes the flesh more tender. *Chermoula* also makes the fish keep longer. If the fish is very large, prick it lightly to allow the marinade to soak into the flesh.

Shrimp are of particular importance for the filling. There are hundreds of different varieties of shrimp. The bodies of these crustaceans grow longer the colder the water is in which they live. When fresh, the small common shrimp have a lovely mild scent, and also smells slightly of iodine. They combine harmoniously with the rice, that is also part of the filling. The rice must be cooked before mixing in the other ingredients.

The sea bass is served with tomatoes, lemons, onions, and bell peppers of various colors. These varieties of vegetable are the ingredients of many Mediterranean dishes.

For the chermoula, place the crushed garlic cloves, chopped parsley, chopped cilantro, chile powder, cumin, and paprika in a bowl. Then pour on vinegar and mix all ingredients. Season with salt and pepper, then stir in tomato paste.

Hold the sea bass by the belly and cut from the head to the tail fins. Lift first 1 fillet, then the other. Loosen and remove the backbone with scissors. Marinate the fish for 2 hours in the chermoula in the fridge.

Peel both lemons. Wash tomatoes and bell peppers and remove seeds from the latter. Cut all fruits into slices, and do the same for the onions. Put aside.

Sea Bass

Blanch the rice for the filling. Add tomato paste, shrimp, and diced pickled lemons, and olives. Add 2 tbsp of chermoula. Dilute the remaining chermoula with a glass of water and put aside.

Carefully stuff the sea bass with the filling. Sew closed using a needle and kitchen thread, starting from the head.

Fill a deep baking pan with slices of tomato, lemon, and onion. Place the sea bass on the slices. Pour on the diluted chermoula, olive oil, and shrimp to garnish. Bake for 40 minutes at 350 °F/180 °C. Then remove thread and serve with vegetables and shrimp.

Monkfish with

Preparation time: 30 minutes
Cooking time: 45 minutes
Difficulty: ★★

Serves 4

1⅓ lbs/600 g	tiger shrimp
1¾ lbs/800 g	monkfish, ready to cook
1⅛ lb/500 g	fresh tomatoes
1⅛ lb/500 g	green bell peppers
1 cup/200 g	rice
1 pinch	saffron threads (as desired)
⅔ oz/20 g	red olives

For the chermoula sauce:

1 bunch	flat-leaf parsley
2 bunches	fresh cilantro (coriander)
2	lemons
2 cloves	garlic
⅓ oz/10 g	ground cumin
1 tbsp	paprika
⅔ oz/20 g	tomato paste
1⅔ cups/400 ml	olive oil
1 splash	white wine vinegar
	salt and pepper

Monkfish medallions with tiger shrimp are on the menus of the best Moroccan restaurants. Monkfish are caught in the deep waters of the Atlantic and the Mediterranean.

This fish is almost never sold in Europe with its head, which is disproportionately large and unattractive. The fish does, however, have the advantage that its cartilaginous spine is easy to remove in one piece. There are no smaller bones in the flesh. The tailpiece provides two fine fillets, also sold separately by the fishmonger.

In order to simplify the recipe introduced here, you can cut the fillets of monkfish into small cubes, marinade them in *chermoula* and then fry them in a pan. The Moroccans also like to brown the fish on skewers. Monkfish ragout in *chermoula* sauce, cooked in a tagine dish, tastes marvelous,

especially served with small pieces of carrot, potato, zucchini, and tomato.

If you can't get monkfish, sea bream or croakers are also suitable for this dish. According to your preferences and the season, you can also add young vegetables.

Choose medium-sized tiger shrimp. In Morocco, there are numerous varieties of shrimp, including common shrimp and the bright red king shrimp.

Rice is an excellent accompaniment to monkfish and can simply be cooked in salt water. Amina Khayar, however, suggests adding a cinnamon stick and a large spoon of butter to the cooking water. Once the rice is drained and colored with the saffron, mix it with the *chermoula*.

Shell the tiger shrimp. Skin the monkfish, remove the backbone, and rinse the fish under running water. Cut the fish into medallions on a cutting board.

For the chermoula, finely chop the parsley and cilantro. Squeeze the lemons. Peel and crush the garlic. Put all the above into a bowl with the cumin, paprika, salt, pepper, tomato paste, oil and vinegar. Stir in cold water until you have created a liquid chermoula.

Scald and skin the tomatoes, cut into halves and de-seed. Cut open the bell peppers, clean and remove seeds. Place the tomatoes and bell peppers in a saucepan. Place the pieces of monkfish on top.

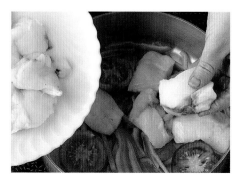

Tiger Shrimp

Pour the chermoula over the fish and the vegetables. Mix well, cover, and cook for 15 minutes on a low heat.

Add the shelled tiger shrimp. Cook for a further 10 minutes. Put part of the chermoula into a small pan and reduce.

Cook the rice. Boil 2 cups of water for 1 cup of rice. Drain and flavor with saffron. Put into a bowl. Pour on reduced chermoula and mix well. Garnish rice and fish with the vegetables and olives and serve.

Preparation time:	25 minutes
Marinating time:	24 hours
Cooking time:	25 minutes
Difficulty:	★★

Serves 4

3 lbs/1.4 kg	pandora
5 oz/150 g	green bell peppers
4½ oz/125 g	red bell peppers
4½ oz/125 g	medium tomatoes
2 tbsp/30 ml	vegetable oil
2 tbsp/30 ml	olive oil
3 oz/75 g	button mushrooms
½ oz/15 g	tomato paste
3 oz/90 g	shelled shrimp
1	pickled lemon

For the chermoula sauce:

2 oz/50 g	fresh cilantro (coriander)
2 oz/50 g	flat-leaf parsley

1 oz/30 g	garlic
7 oz/200 g	onions
¼ tsp	ground cumin
½ tsp	paprika
1	lemon
7 tbsp/100 ml	olive oil
	salt and pepper

For the garnish:

2 oz/50 g	red olives
2 oz/50 g	pickled lemon
⅔ oz/20 g	flat-leaf parsley (as desired)

In many of Morocco's regions, fish are cooked in a sauce of tomatoes, bell peppers, and olive oil. Mohammed Aïtali, who comes from Rabat, has modified these dishes by adding button mushrooms and shrimp to the sauce. His savory and colorful recipe for pandora is, however, reserved for festive occasions. For everyday meals, Moroccans find it sufficient to broil a few economical sardines, small sole, or whiting. Although the chef has decided on pandora, that doesn't mean you can't choose dorade or shi drum.

The delicious *r'bati* fish are supplied by small fishing boats anchoring in front of the old houses of the Oudaïa casbah in Rabat. The Bou Regreg river, which flows into the Atlantic not far away, separates Rabat from the ancient city of Salé. At the mouth of the Bou Regreg, however, there is a maritime "barrier" that has always prevented large ships from entering the harbor. The nearest large port is Casablanca, and most of the fish eaten in Rabat comes from there.

The only mushrooms used in Moroccan cuisine are finely sliced button mushrooms, used equally in fillings for fish and pastries or *briouates*. Wild mushrooms are eaten only rarely. In the markets of the Atlas, the Central Atlas, and the Shoul region (near Rabat), there is, however, a local variety of mushroom on sale, very similar to the button mushroom.

Mohammed Aïtali strongly recommends marinating the fish for a day in the *chermoula* to allow it to develop its full aroma. If you are in a hurry, marinate it for at least an hour. The *chermoula* gives the fine flesh of the pandora a wonderful flavor.

Make a cut in the pandora behind the head at the height of the gills. Carefully lift off the fillets by moving the knife from head to tail along the backbone.

For the chermoula, chop the cilantro, parsley, garlic, and onions and mix with cumin, salt, pepper, and paprika. Add a little lemon juice and a splash of olive oil. Stir to a smooth paste.

Place the fish fillets on a platter. Cover each fillet with chermoula, pressing the marinade down somewhat with the back of a spoon, to allow the fish to take up the aroma. Chill and leave to marinate for 1 day.

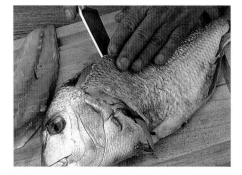

Pandora

On the next day, cut the bell peppers open lengthways. Remove the white pith and the seeds. Halve the tomatoes, remove seeds, and cut into quarters. Cut the bell peppers and tomatoes into thin strips.

Heat a mixture of olive oil and vegetable oil in a pan. Add finely cut bell peppers, tomatoes, and mushrooms and sweat all the above on a high heat, stirring. Add tomato paste mixed with a little water, shrimp, and diced pickled lemon.

Add the marinated fish to the vegetables in the pan. Pour on a little water. Cook in the oven for 15 minutes. Arrange the fish on a bed of vegetables and garnish with red olives, slices of pickled lemon, and parsley.

Jewish-Style

Preparation time: 30 minutes
Cooking time: 25 minutes
Difficulty: ★★

Serves 4

1	pandora, 2¼ lbs/1 kg in weight
1 bunch	cilantro (coriander)
10	ñoras (dried, mild peppers)
6 cloves	garlic
10	thin sticks of reed
7 tbsp/100 ml	vegetable oil
	salt

This Jewish-style fish is typical of Tangier. An inviting family dish, it is usually eaten on Friday evenings at the family meal and was a very widespread dish in earlier times. It was also eaten for lunch as *kemia* on the following day.

Thanks to the balance of its flavors, this dish can also be prepared using dorade. Pandora and dorade, both Mediterranean fish, are suitable for several different methods of cooking.

The pandora can easily be recognized by its shape and is distinguished from the dorade mainly by its reddish coloring. Both fish have white, lean, and very tasty flesh and do not require much cooking. Don't forget to line the bottom of the pan with reeds. This will prevent the fish from sticking.

In this recipe, the cilantro develops its full aroma. The plant is also known as "Arabian parsley" and is used primarily to flavor salads, soups, and sauces. The seeds—coriander—can be recognized by their smell, reminiscent of nutmeg and lemons. Garlic, so prized in those countries bordering on the Mediterranean, is an essential ingredient here. This plant of the onion family can be found all year round in the markets. In spring, buy garlic that is as young as you can get. This is milder and easier to peel. It is best kept in the vegetable compartment of your fridge.

In Morocco, this traditional meal is also known as "fish in red sauce." The color is due to the ñoras—mild peppers from Spain. Christopher Columbus brought these fruits back from the New World and introduced them as a flavoring. The peppers are dried and will keep for at least a year. Don't forget to soak them before using them.

Remove scales from the pandora, gut, and wash. Cut into slices of equal thickness.

Wash the bunch of cilantro and chop finely. Soak the ñoras in cold water.

Peel the cloves of garlic. Crush half of them with a fork and put the others aside.

Fish

Place the stems of reed on the bottom of a pan.

Pour on the oil and the drained ñoras.

Add cilantro and crushed garlic cloves to the pan. Season with salt. Add slices of fish. Mix. Add ½ glass of water and whole garlic cloves. Cook, covered, for 25 minutes. Arrange on a plate and garnish with ñoras and garlic. Pour on a little of the sauce.

Meat & Poultry

Preparation time:	1 hour
Resting time:	30 minutes
Cooking time:	50 minutes
Difficulty:	☆

Serves 4

1 stick	celery
2 pinches	saffron threads
2	lemons
12	small spring artichokes
4½ lbs/2 kg	peas
2	onions
7 tbsp/100 ml	vegetable oil
	salt and pepper

For the meatballs:

1 slice	bread
2¼ lbs/1 kg	ground beef
1	egg
1	onion
1 bunch	parsley
1 pinch	ground ginger
1 tsp	turmeric
1 tsp	mace
1 pinch	nutmeg
	salt and pepper

The Sephardi Jewish community in Morocco, especially in the city of Tangier, has a culinary repertoire rich in Middle Eastern flavors. There are specific dishes for festivals and special occasions.

The Sabbath, the rest day of the week, is on a Saturday and is a day of prayer when families gather together. The celebrations start the evening before: for this occasion the table is covered with a white cloth with two candelabra on it. A carafe of wine, known as the *kiddouch*, is placed on the table, together with *halot* loaves covered by a cloth.

For the Sabbath, which is celebrated with joy and pleasure, many delicious and popular dishes have been developed. People eat heartily on the Sabbath, and religious traditions determine exactly what food is cooked and how it is prepared. Beef meatballs are very popular in Tangier and they are often prepared for the eve of the Sabbath.

The meatballs are made exclusively from kosher meat. The term "kosher" comes from Hebrew and is used for foodstuffs that can be eaten without any problems complying with the religious rules. A celery sauce or peas and artichokes are served as an accompaniment.

The meat, mixed with parsley, onion, egg, bread, mace, nutmeg, ginger, turmeric, and salt and pepper, is very aromatic. If you decide to make a celery sauce, take the meat out of the sauce and reduce it. You can also make the meatballs with lamb.

For the meatballs, soak the bread in water. In a bowl, mix the meat with the soaked bread and the egg. Add chopped onion, finely chopped parsley, ginger, turmeric, mace, and nutmeg. Season with salt and pepper.

Mix all ingredients using your fingers, then allow to rest for 30 minutes. Meanwhile, wash the celery. Cut the stick into fine matchsticks and put aside, with the pulled-off leaves. Mix the saffron threads with 1½ glasses of water.

With moistened hands, form evenly sized meatballs. Squeeze the 2 lemons and put the juice into a bowl with cold water. Remove the leaves of the artichokes down to the bottom. Remove the fibers and put the artichoke bottoms in water.

Meatballs

Shell the peas. Peel the onions and sweat in 2 tbsp of vegetable oil. Pour on ½ glass of saffron water. Add the peas and artichoke bottoms. Season with salt and pepper. Cover all the above with water and cook for 10–15 minutes.

Place half the meatballs into a pan. Pour on 3 tbsp of vegetable oil and ½ glass of saffron water. Cook, covered, for about 15 minutes.

Place the celery in a pan. Add the remaining meatballs, 2 tbsp oil, and the remaining saffron water. Season. Cover with celery leaves. Cook for 20 minutes. Arrange the meatballs on a serving platter alongside the meatballs cooked with peas and artichokes.

Sous-Style

Preparation time: 30 minutes
Marinating time: 30 minutes
Cooking: on the barbecue
Difficulty: ★

Serves 4

1⅓ lb/600 g	chicken breast fillets
1	green lime
1	onion
½ bunch	fresh cilantro (coriander)
2 cloves	garlic
2 tbsp/30 ml	argan oil

1 tbsp	ras el-hanout (spice mixture)
1 pinch	saffron threads
	salt and pepper

For the tapenade:

3½ oz/100 g	green pitted olives
1	pickled lemon
1 tbsp/15 ml	argan oil

These chicken skewers are typical of the region around Agadir. This coastal resort, capital of the Sous region, lies on the Atlantic coast and is distinguished by a rich and varied cuisine.

In this recipe, the white chicken meat is cooked on a charcoal barbecue. If you don't have the opportunity of barbecuing in the open air, the chef recommends using a frying pan. If this is the case, heat two tablespoons of olive oil and fry the chicken meat on high heat on both sides. Then, using long wooden skewers, put into the oven for five minutes at 350 °F/180 °C.

Thanks to the marinade, the chicken skewers are very aromatic and the meat is tender and easier to keep. Each of the ingredients used contributes to the taste of the dish with its own specific flavor.

Argan oil, very popular in Morocco, is produced exclusively in the Sous region. It is made from the fruits of the argan tree, which grows wild, and is distinguished by a strong, nutty taste. The people of Agadir use the oil frequently, particularly combined with bread for breakfast. The chef claims that women also use the oil cosmetically, as it gives them a wonderfully delicate and glowing complexion.

For this marinade with a Middle Eastern flavor, the famous *ras el-hanout* is used. The name of this mixture of ground spices, root bark, and dried flowers means "head of the spice dealer." In other words, *ras el-hanout* is an individual combination of spices. The mixture does indeed vary according to origin and the traditions in question, and which spices are used depends not least on the budget of the customer.

Trim excess fat from the chicken breasts as desired. Cut the meat into equal-sized cubes.

Squeeze the green lime. Peel the onion and chop finely. Chop the cilantro and cloves of garlic.

In a bowl, mix cubes of chicken, finely chopped onion, chopped garlic cloves, cilantro, and the juice of the green lime. Add argan oil. Season with salt and pepper. Add ras el-hanout and saffron threads. Marinate for 30 minutes.

Chicken Skewers

For the tapenade, chop the olives in a food processor.

Add the peel of the pickled lemon and mix again. Beat the tapenade with the argan oil and then put aside.

Thread the cubes of chicken onto skewers and cook on the barbecue. Serve with the tapenade.

Quails with

Preparation time:	40 minutes
Cooking time	
for quails:	30 minutes
Cooking time	
for couscous:	1 hour
Difficulty:	★★

Serves 4

8	quails
9 oz/250 g	onions
1/3 oz/10 g	garlic
1/3 oz/10 g	flat-leaf parsley
1/3 oz/10 g	fresh cilantro (coriander)
1 pinch	saffron threads
1 pinch	ground cinnamon
5½ tbsp/80 ml	olive oil
1 splash	orange flower water
	salt and pepper

For the filling:

2 1/3 cups/400 g	couscous semolina
1 splash	olive oil
7 oz/200 g	slivered almonds
1 tsp/5 g	ground cinnamon
2 oz/50 g	caster sugar
1 splash	orange flower water
	salt

For the garnish:

| 2 oz/50 g | slivered almonds |
| 1 oz/30 g | fresh cilantro (coriander) (as desired) |

In Morocco, there are many delicious and rich dishes with quails. Mohammed Aïtali simmers the quails in a bouillon flavored with herbs, onion, and saffron. He then fills them with a heavenly stuffing made from crushed roasted almonds, sugar, semolina, cinnamon, and orange flower water. As a precaution, fry the quails first on the side where they have the most meat, not necessarily, therefore, on the breast side. They are turned later.

In Morocco, quails are particularly prized among gourmets. Among the finest creations of the chefs from Fez, famed for their sophisticated dishes, is the quail *pastilla* with almonds, liberally sprinkled with icing sugar and cinnamon. Quails are also cooked with roast almonds, chicken livers, or a mixture of fine noodles, cinnamon, and orange flower water.

Many festive dishes in Morocco contain almonds or raisins, symbols of luxury and wealth. Stuffed quails, *tajines*, *mêchouis*, and *pastillas* are unthinkable without these two ingredients. The region around Agadir, with its hot climate, is famous for the quality of the almonds grown there, known in Moroccan as *louz*. They are hardly ever used fresh, but when dried they enrich many dishes.

The large Moroccan *louz* are much less in demand than the sweet, small *bled* almonds. Blanched or slivered (flaked) almonds are best for quail filling. Slivered almonds are easier to roast and chop.

For the filling, place couscous semolina in a shallow bowl and work in a little oil and water by hand. Pour the grains into the strainer on the top of a couscous steamer. Steam 3 times for 20 minutes at a time; between steaming stages, work in a little salt and water.

Cut off the necks of the quails. Clean the birds, then rinse them, and dab dry from the inside with kitchen paper. Trim off the wingtips.

Peel and chop the onions and garlic and also chop the parsley and cilantro. Put a splash of oil and one of orange flower water, the chopped herbs, and the quails into a pan. Sprinkle with saffron, cinnamon, salt and pepper. Cover with water. Cook for 30 minutes on a high heat.

Almond Stuffing

Dry-roast the slivered almonds in a frying pan. Chop in a food processor. Mix well with cinnamon and sugar. Put the cooked couscous into a bowl and fold the almond mixture in thoroughly with a spoon.

Sprinkle the mixture with orange flower water. Mix with a spoon until a brown, homogeneous mass is formed.

Take the quails out of the cooking liquid and allow to cool slightly. Fill the quails with the stuffing. Dry-roast the slivered almonds for the garnish without adding fat. Serve the quails in the cooking liquid sprinkled with roast slivers of almond and garnished with cilantro.

Arab–Berber-Style

Preparation time: 1 hour
Marinating time: 1 hour
Resting time: 1 hour 5 minutes
Cooking time
    for semolina: 20 minutes
Difficulty: ★★

Serves 4

2 tbsp/30 ml   vegetable oil
               oil for frying

M'ssemen pastry:
4⅓ cups/500 g   flour
                 salt

Berber method:
9 oz/250 g   lamb hearts
½ bunch   parsley

½ bunch   cilantro (coriander)
2 tsp   ground cumin
2   onions, chopped
3 tbsp/45 ml   vegetable oil
               salt and white pepper

Arab method:
9 oz/250 g   lamb hearts
2 tbsp/30 ml   vegetable oil
2 tsp   ground cumin
½ bunch   parsley
½ bunch   cilantro (coriander)
1   egg
               salt and white pepper

Morocco is a wonderful country of contrasts. Ethnic variety and regional characteristics have had a major effect on the culinary tradition. In Morocco, you can find innumerable methods of cooking a single ingredient. With this recipe, Abdellah Achiai wanted to honor both the Berber and the Arab population, and therefore describes two methods of cooking lamb's hearts.

The Berbers, the original inhabitants of Morocco, are especially partial to skewered grilled meats. In the south of the country, families from the isolated villages, known as *douars*, go to the market once a week. The way to the city is long and is undertaken on the back of a donkey or on small rattling wagons even in great heat. But it is well worth the effort, as the market is a general meeting-place, where people meet their friends and relations.

Amongst family and friends, news is exchanged, and the traditional lamb's heart skewers are enjoyed. They are eaten directly at the stand where they have been bought. This dish is associated with social gatherings.

Among the Arab population, lamb's hearts, a specialty of the Atlas Mountains, are also highly prized. In Arab cuisine, lamb's hearts are used to fill envelopes of pastry, so-called *m'ssemen*. The pastry consists of flour, water, and a little salt, and is made into little balls. These are rolled out on a well-oiled surface, covered with filling, and then carefully folded. The chef recommends frying the *m'ssemen* on both sides. The Arabs in the south of the country also eat *m'ssemen* for breakfast, with coffee and milk.

For the m'ssemen pastry, place flour and salt into a bowl. Gradually add water. Knead with your hands. Let the finished dough rest for 5 minutes.

Place the pastry on a well-oiled surface. Take a little in your hand and press it out between thumb and forefinger so little balls are formed. Place the balls on a baking tray, cover with a cloth and allow to rest for 1 hour.

For the Berber style, chop the lamb's hearts into large cubes, for the Arab style chop them into small cubes. For the Berber style marinade, mix finely chopped parsley and cilantro, cumin, onions, oil, salt and pepper in a bowl. Marinate the hearts in the mixture for 1 hour.

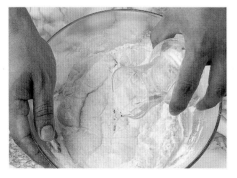

Lamb Hearts

For the filling for the Arab method, fry the lamb's hearts in a little vegetable oil. Season with salt and pepper. Add cumin, finely chopped parsley, and cilantro. Cook for about 10 minutes. Add the beaten egg and stir all ingredients.

Roll out the balls of pastry on the oiled surface. Cover with the filling. Carefully fold the pastry over to make triangular envelopes. Fry the m'ssemen in a pan in for 8–10 minutes. Drain.

For the Berber method, thread the marinated cubes of lamb's hearts onto skewers and broil or grill on a barbecue. Arrange both dishes and serve.

Steamed Shoulder

Preparation time:	35 minutes
Cooking time:	50 minutes
Difficulty:	★★

Serves 8

4	shoulders of lamb, each 2¼ lbs/1 kg
6	carrots
2	onions
2	leeks
1 tbsp	ground cumin
1 tbsp	fine salt

1 bunch	parsley
1 bunch	cilantro (coriander)
1 tbsp	olive oil
5 oz/150 g	small potatoes
5 oz/150 g	turnips
5 oz/150 g	small onions
5 oz/150 g	green beans
7 oz/200 g	peas
12	violet artichokes
6	zucchini

Pastry:

| ⁷⁄₈ cup/100 g | flour |
| 2 | eggs |

In Morocco, shoulder of lamb is often cooked in the strainer on top of a couscous steamer. The result is tender meat, permeated through and through by the aroma of cumin and fresh vegetables. This dish is often made for *Aid el-kebir*, the festival when Abraham's sacrifice is remembered. On this occasion some families cook up to two whole sheep to feed their guests. Officially, the festival only lasts for a day, but there are so many recipes for this occasion that celebrations last for at least a week.

Many different kinds of vegetable are cultivated in Morocco. Potatoes in particular, as Amina Khayar knows, are very popular among the regional varieties. Moroccans especially prize the small violet-colored potatoes, which cook firmly and keep their shape.

Peas are among the most commonly eaten vegetables. For example, they are used in the *m'kader* lamb tagine together with potatoes, red olives, and pickled lemons.

As a rule, Moroccan cooks use a piece of cloth to cover the join between both parts of a couscous steamer. The material is kneaded with a little flour and water to allow the least possible amount of steam to escape from the pot. Amina Khayar has chosen a simpler method, but in either case the seal hardens as soon as the couscous steamer becomes hot.

Always offer salt and cumin with this dish, to allow all the guests to adjust seasoning for themselves. The aroma of the spices rubbed into the meat disappears in the steam during the cooking process.

Open up the shoulder of lamb. Remove as much as possible of the small membranes and excess fat.

Peel 2 carrots and the onions, clean 1 leek and cut into large pieces. Fill the couscous steamer three-quarters full with water. Add the vegetables and bring everything to the boil.

Rub the shoulder of lamb with salt and cumin. Line the strainer of the couscous steamer with parsley and cilantro and place the meat on top. Pour on olive oil. Place the strainer on top of the pot.

# of Lamb

Prepare the pastry to seal the couscous steamer. Mix the flour with 2 egg whites in a bowl. Knead with the fingers until you have a smooth elastic dough.

Place the dough over the join of pot and strainer. Cover and cook for 30 minutes. Meanwhile, peel the small potatoes, the remaining carrots, the turnips, and onions.

Clean the second leek, prepare the green beans, and shell the peas. Remove the artichoke leaves and cut the zucchini into sticks. Put all vegetables on top of the meat. Cover and cook for another 20 minutes.

Shoulder of Lamb

Preparation time: 25 minutes
Cooking time: 1 hour 5 minutes
Difficulty: ★★

Serves 4

²/₃ cup/100 g	dried apricots
2	shoulders of lamb
4 tbsp/60 ml	peanut oil
2	onions
3 sticks	cinnamon
¹/₂ tsp/2 g	saffron threads
¹/₂ envelope	Moroccan saffron powder for coloring

2 tbsp/30 ml	olive oil
¹/₂ tsp	ground ginger
1 bunch	fresh parsley
1 bunch	fresh cilantro (coriander)
⁴/₅ cup/150 g	prunes
1	lemon
¹/₄ cup/50 g	sugar
¹/₂ stick/40 g	butter
	salt and pepper

Shoulder of lamb, or *delaa* in Arabic, is top of the list of favorite Moroccan dishes. The chef here cooks it in a rich saffron sauce and further refines it with cinnamon, lemon, poached prunes, and apricots cooked in butter. If desired, it can also be cooked with prunes stuffed with nuts, artichokes, and peas.

One shoulder of lamb is considered to serve two people. Before cooking, the meat is rinsed thoroughly to meet the requirements of religious rules. An animal slaughtered according to the Muslim *hallal* rite has to be completely free of blood, as blood is considered unclean.

Do not forget to score the surface of the shoulder of lamb lightly, so that the shallow cuts form criss-cross lines. This helps the meat to cook and makes it easier to carve once it is done. Bouchaïb Kama also pricks the meat several times

in different places with the point of the knife to allow the spices to penetrate better and to allow the aroma and flavor to soak thorough into the meat. If you wish to brown the shoulder of lamb to make it more attractive and crispy, complete the cooking process in the oven on the highest temperature.

Apricots are grown on a large scale in Morocco and are the most widespread fruit in the country. They are either preserved in syrup or dried. Fresh apricots are often eaten with cinnamon, honey, and orange flower water as a dessert. Dried, they are rarely used in savory dishes, except for lamb tagines. Prunes are also added to mutton or beef dishes in Morocco. In earlier times, *gasaa* couscous, garnished with prunes and hard-boiled eggs, was served to newlyweds after the wedding night.

Soak the apricots in a bowl with lukewarm water. Rinse the shoulders of lamb. Score lightly with a knife to make a criss-cross pattern of cuts.

Heat 2 tbsp of peanut oil in a large saucepan. Add chopped onions, 2 cinnamon sticks, saffron threads and powder, salt and pepper. Sweat over a high heat. Turn the shoulders of lamb several times to cover them completely with the spices.

Pour 2 tbsp of olive oil and 2 tbsp of peanut oil over the meat and dust with ginger. Cover with water and cook for 30 minutes.

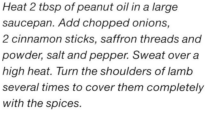

with Apricots

At the end of this cooking period, scatter chopped parsley and chopped cilantro over the meat. Cook for at least another 30 minutes.

Prepare the prunes: place some water, 1 cinnamon stick, slices of lemon, sugar, and the prunes into a saucepan. Poach until the prunes are soft. Drain the apricots and sauté in ¼ stick/20 g butter.

Place the lamb on a serving platter. Simmer the meat juices and reduce on a high heat. Add the rest of the butter and stir in well, then continue to reduce. Cover the meat with the sauce and garnish with apricots and prunes.

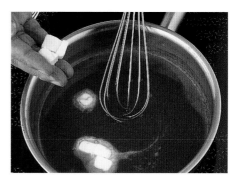

Shank of Veal

Preparation time:	30 minutes
Cooking time:	1 hour 5 minutes
Difficulty:	✶

Serves 4

2	lemons
5	fennel bulbs
3 tbsp/45 ml	vegetable oil
2¼ lb/1 kg	shank of veal
1	onion
4 cloves	garlic
1 bunch	parsley
1 bunch	cilantro (coriander)

½ tsp	ginger
1 pinch	saffron threads
2	tomatoes, skinned
	salt and pepper

For the filling:

5 oz/150g	ground beef
1	onion
	fennel leaves
	salt and pepper

For the garnish (as desired):

	fresh dill

Shank of veal with fennel is a traditional dish, eaten mainly in the Casablanca region. It is easy to prepare and full of the aromas of the Mediterranean.

Fennel, *besbes* in Arabic, grows all over the country. The umbeliferous plant is easy to recognize by its aniseed-like scent. It grows to a height of up to six feet and thrives especially in the sandy soils of the coastal region.

Fennel is a winter vegetable, and the stalks, twigs, and seeds can all be eaten. The scent of the bulbs becomes a little milder with cooking. Fennel essence contains around 85 percent anethol, the same as aniseed. Choose small fennel bulbs, as these are much more tender than the large ones. Don't forget to keep the aniseed-flavored green leaves growing from the ends of the stalks. The chef uses them for the filling.

The shank of veal should simmer for some time. This part of the leg, directly under the knee, is very tasty. Choose good quality, first class veal.

The aromatic parsley, cilantro, and garlic give the dish a wonderful flavor. The pinch of ginger, which gives the meat that special touch, is essential. This spicy root from India and Malaysia is frequently used in Middle Eastern cooking and has many medicinal properties. Its aromatic tuber is eaten fresh, preserved, and ground.

Saffron, cultivated in Talioune, a little village in southern Morocco, between Ouarzazate and Taradouant, gives the dish a strong color and delicate scent. This spice was brought to Spain by the Moors. The pollen stamens of the purple crocus are mixed with water before being added to the other ingredients.

Squeeze the lemons and pour the juice into a bowl, adding a little water. Cut off the ends of the fennel bulbs. From four of them, take off the leaves until you reach the heart and place everything into the bowl. Chop the fifth bulb very finely.

For the filling, mix the ground beef with finely chopped onion and chopped fennel leaves. Season with salt and pepper.

Stuff the fennel leaves with the ground beef mixture. Keep cool.

with Fennel

In the vegetable oil briefly fry the shank of veal that has been cut into pieces. Add finely chopped onion and fennel, crushed garlic cloves, parsley and cilantro (both finely chopped). Season with salt and pepper, ginger and saffron. Fry for 10 minutes.

Cover the meat with water. Cook for 40 minutes with the lid closed. Half-way through the cooking period add the skinned tomatoes, chopped into small cubes.

Place the filled fennel in the pan. On a very low heat, cook for about 15 minutes. Arrange the shank of veal with the stuffed fennel and garnish with dill.

Chicken

Preparation time:	*45 minutes*
Cooking time:	*40 minutes*
Difficulty:	★★

Serves 4

8	chicken fillets, 5 oz/140 g each
8	chicken thighs
1 bunch	parsley
1 bunch	cilantro (coriander)
	salt and pepper

2 pinches	saffron threads
2 large	onions
4 cloves	garlic
1 tbsp/15 ml	olive oil
1 tbsp/15 ml	peanut oil
½ envelope	Moroccan saffron powder for coloring
⅓ oz/10 g	ginger
11 oz/320 g	button mushrooms
11 oz/320 g	spring onions
2 cups/500 ml	chicken stock
½ stick/40 g	butter

Kourdass are a type of roulade, already invented by the forefathers of the Moroccans. In the traditional recipe, the filling is made from liver and heart of lamb, herbs, and spices, held together with lamb tripe. Bouchaïb Kama has adapted it to modern eating habits and uses chicken. His filling is a delicate combination of chicken, parsley, cilantro, and saffron, rolled up in chicken fillet beaten very thin. Other chefs are no less inventive and also make *kourdass* with fish.

In Morocco, chicken and lamb are eaten with about the same frequency. Many poultry farms have been set up between Casablanca and Rabat, where most of the consumers live, so poultry is now much more economical. It is also less fatty than lamb, as all Moroccans who are watching their weight know.

For this recipe, you should use the ready-to-cook fillets and boned thighs of four whole small chickens. After cutting off and boning fillets and thighs, make your own stock out of the carcasses. Put them into a pan with parsley stems, finely chopped onions, carrots, and twigs of thyme. Cover with water and cook for one to one and a half hours. You can, of course, prepare your *kourdass* with instant chicken stock. If after the preparation you still have some filling left over, make it into little meatballs in a tomato and herb sauce.

Our chef adds button mushrooms to the sauce. The mushrooms are locally produced: they grow in Imouzar in the Atlas Mountains in caves. All the mushrooms known in Europe also grow in the undergrowth of Moroccan forests: chanterelles, hedgehogs, morels, and ceps.

Place a chicken fillet on a piece of plastic wrap. Cover with a second piece of plastic wrap and beat until flat. Do the same to the other fillets.

Bone the chicken thighs. Place the meat on a chopping board. First dice, then grind finely in a food processor.

Add salt, pepper, half the chopped parsley, and half the chopped cilantro plus 1 pinch of saffron threads. Mix by hand until the mixture is smooth.

Kourdass

Put a little of the filling on the end of a fillet. Roll up to make a roulade. Fasten the ends with a wooden toothpick. Prepare another 7 kourdass in the same way. Peel and chop onions and garlic.

Fry onions and garlic briefly in olive and peanut oil. Add kourdass and turn while frying. Add 1 pinch saffron threads and the saffron powder, and also ginger, cilantro, parsley, quartered mushrooms, and peeled spring onions.

Cook the kourdass for about 40 minutes until tender, gradually adding the chicken stock. Once the kourdass are cooked, reduce the sauce and beat in butter. Halve each kourdass and serve in the sauce with the onions.

Rabbit with

Preparation time:	25 minutes
Cooking time:	1 hour 10 minutes
Difficulty:	✷✷

Serves 4

1	rabbit, 4½ lbs/2 kg
4 tbsp/60 ml	olive oil
2 envelopes	Moroccan saffron powder for coloring

1 tsp/5 g	ginger
7 oz/200 g	onions
1 bunch	parsley
1 bunch	cilantro (coriander)
2¼ lbs/1 kg	Swiss chard
1	fresh lemon
	salt and pepper

Rabbit meat is much esteemed, especially in southern Morocco, and is often steamed. In Marrakesh, chefs sometimes use the thighs in a *tangia*, a kind of ragout, simmered for a long time in an amphora-like container. M'hamed Chahid has decided to cook the rabbit in a sauce of onions, ginger, and herbs, to which he adds Swiss chard stalks.

The recipe he presents here is based on a dish with a long tradition in Morocco: hare with wild cardoon thistle. In the mountains, it is easy to catch one of the many hares that live there. In most countries, however, hares are available only in the hunting season. It is therefore easier to replace them with rabbit.

Swiss chard belongs to the same botanical family as spinach. In his restaurant, the chef generally prefers to use wild cardoon thistle with its prickly stems and slightly bitter taste.

The leaves and stems of Swiss chard are edible. The latter replace the cardoon thistle in this dish. You can, however, also vary the recipe a little by replacing them with okra or even with small, sour-flavored quince. The cut-off green chard leaves can be cooked like spinach.

In Moroccan cooking, vegetables are a dish in themselves and by no means only an accompaniment. Respecting this tradition, M'hamed Chahid cuts the Swiss chard stems into pieces and cooks them in the meat sauce. This makes them an integral part of the meal and they deliciously absorb the flavors of the herbs and spices.

Remove the head of the rabbit and trim excess fat. Cut the body into 6 or 8 pieces using a carving knife.

Heat some oil in a pan and place the rabbit pieces in it. Season with saffron powder, ginger, salt and pepper. Add peeled and chopped onions.

Chop the parsley and cilantro and add to the pan. Allow to fry for about 10 minutes. Cover with water, cover the pan and cook gently for 45 minutes on a low heat.

Swiss Chard Stems

Cut the Swiss chard leaves off the stems. Clean the stems and scrape with a knife to remove fibers.

Halve the chard stems lengthways, then cut into sticks. Rinse with plenty of water and then place in water mixed with lemon juice.

At the end of the cooking period, add the chard stems to the rabbit sauce. Pour on a little water. Cover the pan and cook for a further 15 minutes.

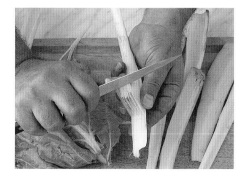

M'rouzia

Preparation time: 25 minutes
Soaking time: overnight
Cooking time: 1 hour 55 minutes
Difficulty: ☆

Serves 6

1½ cups/250 g	golden raisins
2¼ lbs/1 kg each	shank, shoulder, and leg of lamb
4	onions
2 tbsp	ground ginger

1 pinch	saffron threads
1 pinch	Moroccan saffron powder for coloring
2 tbsp	smen (preserved butter)
2 tbsp	honey
2 cups/500 ml	oil
1½ cups/200 g	blanched almonds

This lamb dish, known as *m'rouzia*, was created behind the fortifications of the ancient city of Fez. Before there were fridges, this method of cooking allowed the meat to be kept for several months. After spices and preserved butter (*smen*) had been added, the pieces of mutton or lamb were simmered for many hours over the coals of the *m'jmar*, a charcoal oven. After that, all the ingredients were placed in a terracotta container: the meat right at the bottom, the raisins and almonds above and finally the sauce. When cooling, the sauce would set, forming a protective layer covering the meat. Finally, the container was covered with a piece of oiled paper tied down with cord.

Today, *m'rouzia* is often prepared for *'Aid el-kebir*. At this festival, Moroccans eat a great deal of mutton and lamb. Nowadays, however, the meat is cooked in a pan over a gas flame. *M'rouzia* can be kept for three or four months in large glass jars in the fridge.

The flavors of *m'rouzia* can be varied according to personal taste. Many people season it with cinnamon or *ras el-hanout* (a Moroccan spice mixture), or with dried and ground coriander. It is sweetened with either sugar or honey. The chef definitely prefers the latter, as the honey holds the meat together better, and gives it a glaze and an attractive golden-brown color.

Not everyone likes the intense flavor of *smen*, which can be replaced by olive oil. To make *smen*, butter is first allowed to soften at room temperature. Then, over a period of one and a half hours, fine salt and hot water are worked into it on a plate. In an airtight Mason jar, *smen* will keep for several years.

Soak the raisins the evening before in a bowl of cold water. Cut the shank, shoulder and leg of lamb into large pieces.

Peel the onions and cut into very thin slices.

Place the meat in a large saucepan. Cover with finely sliced onions. Add ginger, saffron threads, saffron powder, and smen. Brown for 10–15 minutes, turning the pieces of meat from time to time.

from Fez

Pour water over the meat until the pan is three-quarters full. Cover. Cook for 1 hour 30 minutes, until the meat begins to loosen off the bones.

Towards the end of the cooking time, add the honey and the drained raisins to the meat. Stir. Cook for another 5–10 minutes, until the sauce has a slightly syrupy consistency.

In a pan, fry the blanched almonds in the oil. Sprinkle the almonds over the meat and serve.

Pastilla

Preparation time:	*1 hour*
Cooking time:	*1 hour 15 minutes*
Difficulty:	★★

Serves 4

1⅛ lb/500 g	onions
4	pigeons, each 1lb/450 g
1½ sticks/150 g	butter
½ tsp	ground ginger
1 tbsp	ground cinnamon
1 pinch	saffron threads
1 bunch	parsley
1 bunch	cilantro (coriander)

1	cinnamon stick
1 tbsp	orange flower water
⅞ cup/200 g	sugar
10	eggs
1¾ cups/250 g	blanched almonds
1⅛ lb/500 g	*yufka* pastry dough sheets
	salt and pepper

For the garnish:

	powdered sugar
	ground cinnamon
	almonds
	mint leaves (as desired)

Recipes for *pastilla*, which are widespread and exist in many versions, clearly demonstrate the sophistication of Moroccan cuisine. Depending on the family recipe, *pastillas* are made with chicken, offal, or fish. However marvelous they all taste, they pale in comparison with pigeon *pastilla*, the most delicious and most famous of all *pastilla* recipes. However, you do need some time and patience to make this dish.

According to Lahoussine Bel Moufid, Moroccans feel a positively emotional tie to *pastilla* or *ourqa* dough. It is made from flour, water, and salt and reached the country some 1,300 years ago with the Arab conquerors. It originally came from Isfahan in Persia, but it was the Arabs who over the centuries influenced Moroccan cuisine. Brush the sheets of dough with butter while you work with them. This prevents the dough from drying out.

The *pastilla* grants the pigeon a place of honor. Pigeons are highly prized in Morocco because of their meat. In Arabic, the pigeon is known as *hamam* and represents cunning and subtlety. The almonds in this dish are irreplaceable. Almonds originated in Asia. The fruits of the almond tree contain one or two nuts surrounded by a hard shell. Dried, almonds are a common ingredient in Middle Eastern dishes.

The presentation of this dish is also part of its charm. The *pastilla* is always sprinkled with powdered sugar and cinnamon, adding an extra refined touch. It is indeed the garnish that distinguishes this luxurious dish. Many chefs, such as Lahoussine Bel Moufid, become true artists with this task. For example, you can make a flower out of almonds in the center of the *pastilla* and garnish this with leaves of mint.

Peel the onions and slice finely. Cut the pigeon into pieces. In a large pot, sweat the onions in ½ stick/50 g of butter. Add the pieces of pigeon, ginger, ground cinnamon, saffron threads, salt and pepper. Pour on 2 cups/500 ml of water and cook for 30–40 minutes.

Add finely chopped parsley and cilantro, as well as the cinnamon stick, orange flower water, and ⅔ cup/150 g sugar. Cook for 10 minutes. Take out and bone the pigeon pieces. Reduce the sauce for about 15 minutes. Beat 8 eggs and stir in.

Dry-roast the almonds without adding fat, and crush them. Melt the rest of the butter and brush a round baking dish with some of it. Cover with 1 sheet of yufka pastry dough. Place 4 further sheets in a rosette pattern, overlapping slightly. Brush with a little melted butter.

with Pigeon

Put in the pigeon meat. Add the sauce with the eggs, then add the almonds. Sprinkle with the remaining sugar.

Separate the 2 remaining eggs and keep the yolks. Cover the pastilla with 2 sheets of yufka pastry dough. Fold over the protruding edges and brush with egg yolk.

Place one last sheet of pastry dough on top and stick down with egg yolk. Bake in the oven, between 2 baking trays, for 10 minutes at 350 °F/180 °C. Drizzle butter over the pastilla and sprinkle with powdered sugar and cinnamon. Garnish with almonds and mint leaves.

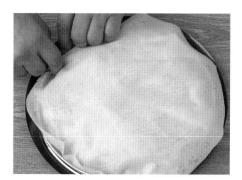

Pigeon

Preparation time: 40 minutes
Cooking time: 1 hour 10 minutes
Difficulty: ☆

Serves 4

4	squab pigeons, 1 lb/450 g each
⅔ cup/150 ml	olive oil
1 tsp	*smen* (preserved butter) or salted butter
8	eggs
½ bunch	parsley
1 tbsp/15 ml	vegetable oil
	salt and pepper

For the marinade:

½ bunch	parsley
½ bunch	fresh cilantro (coriander)
4 cloves	garlic
9 oz/250 g	onions
1 pinch	saffron threads
½ tsp/3 g	mastic gum
1 tsp	ground ginger
	salt and pepper

For the garnish:

2	pickled lemons
	purple olives (as desired)

In Moroccan, *m'fenede* more or less means hidden or concealed. You simply have to try this dish to discover the pigeon hidden under the omelet. In the mountains of the High Atlas in southern Morocco, or more precisely in Tafilalet and Sijilmassa, this dish is offered to young mothers in particular. Pigeon *m'fenede* is a highly symbolic dish, and it is said that it improves mother's milk and thereby encourages the growth of the newborn infant. To keep up the tradition, some Moroccans even today serve the dish to a woman shortly after birth.

Pigeon *m'fenede* is also part of the heritage of fine cuisine in Morocco and is therefore frequently cooked for ceremonial occasions. The tender flesh of the pigeons and their delicious taste make them an ideal ingredient for luxury dishes. Wild pigeons can be found in the markets from spring to the end of summer; for the rest of the year,

you will have to be content with farmed pigeons. You can, however, make this recipe using other poultry such as chicken, for example.

There are various methods for preparing pigeon *m'fenede*. Khadija Bensdira suggests simply folding the pigeon into a fine omelet just before serving. Others prefer to cook the pigeons first in hot oil, and to then take them out and dip them in beaten egg before frying them again. The third method, inherited from the Alawit dynasty, is the most difficult. The pigeon is put in a large pan with a little sauce. When it is hot, beaten eggs are added and the pot is covered once again. As soon as the pigeon is cooked, it must be removed from the pan without the protective layer of egg falling off. However you prepare the pigeons, the intention is that your guests must not suspect what is hidden in the omelet!

In a bowl, prepare the marinade from chopped parsley, chopped cilantro, crushed cloves of garlic, and finely diced onion. Add saffron threads, mastic gum, and ground ginger. Season with salt and pepper. Pour on a little water.

Hold the pigeons over an open flame to singe off any remaining down. Cut off the feet and the tips of the wings. Gut the pigeons and rinse under running water. Tie the thighs and wings tightly to the body with kitchen twine.

Place the pigeons in the marinade. Cut the pickled lemons into pieces and put aside for the garnish.

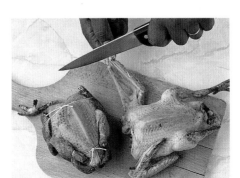

M'fenede

In a saucepan, bring the pigeons to the boil in the marinade. Cover with water. When this boils, add olive oil and smen. Turn the pigeons. Cook for about 1 hour, then take out the pigeons and reduce the sauce.

Place the pigeons in the oven for about 3 minutes at 350 °F/180 °C. Break the eggs and beat with the chopped parsley. Season with salt and pepper. Fry 4 omelets in oil in a frying pan.

Untie the twine from the pigeons and wrap each pigeon in an omelet. Arrange on plates. Garnish with pieces of pickled lemon and purple olives.

Chicken

Preparation time: 40 minutes
Marinating time: 1 hour
Cooking time: 40 minutes
Difficulty: ★

Serves 4

1	chicken weighing 2½ lbs/1.2 kg
6 tbsp/90 ml	vegetable oil
1⅛ lb/500 g	onions
1¾ cups/250 g	blanched almonds
	salt

For the marinade:

1 bunch	parsley
1 tbsp	red food coloring
1 tsp	saffron threads
1 tsp	*smen* (preserved butter) or olive oil
4 tbsp/60 ml	vegetable oil
	salt and white pepper

For the garnish:

	parsley

In Moroccan cooking, the term *kedra* refers to a specific method of cooking based on cooked onions and almonds. In the Fez area, chicken is usually served with this slightly sweet accompaniment.

This traditional and sophisticated dish is generally eaten at the family table. According to Abdellah Achiai, even today it is almost always prepared by grandmothers. It is easy to cook, but does take some time.

Many Moroccans are very choosy when it comes to picking the right chicken. All over the country, the *beldi* free-range chickens that can be recognized by their multi-colored feathers are highly prized. On market days, farmers from the surrounding villages make their way to town, loaded down with cages in which they transport their live chickens.

Gourmets in the market choose their *beldi* chicken, which is slaughtered and plucked on the spot. For this recipe, choose a free-range chicken with firm flesh and little fat. These chickens usually need to cook for some time.

The *kedra*, made from onions, is used as a flavoring but also eaten as a vegetable, and is typically Moroccan. The onions have a sweetish flavor if grown in a sunny place. This bulb, of the lily family, has been cultivated for 5,000 years and originated in northern Asia. Choose onions that are not sprouting, with a firm, hard bulb.

The almonds in the onion mixture also come from Asia. The Romans knew them as "Greek nuts." You should use blanched almonds for this recipe.

Cut off the wings and legs of the chicken and divide the body into 2 parts. Cut off the fillets.

For the marinade, place chopped parsley, food coloring, saffron threads, and smen in a bowl. Pour in the oil. Season with salt and pepper. Marinate the chicken pieces for 1 hour.

Fry the chicken pieces briefly in the marinade and 1 tbsp vegetable oil. Cover with water and cook for about 30 minutes.

Kedra

Peel the onions and slice thinly. Cook slowly in the rest of the vegetable oil on a low heat. Season with salt.

Once the chicken is cooked, place aside. Blanch the almonds for about 10 minutes in boiling water.

Place the almonds in the saucepan with the onions and stir carefully. Arrange the chicken meat with the accompaniment on plates. Garnish with chopped parsley.

Oxtail

Preparation time: 20 minutes
Soaking time: overnight
Cooking time: 2 hours 15 minutes
Difficulty: ☆

Serves 4

1¼ cups/200 g	garbanzo beans (chickpeas)
4 tbsp/60 ml	vegetable oil
4 tbsp/60 ml	olive oil
3 lbs/1.4 kg	oxtail, in pieces
⅔ oz/20 g	flat-leaf parsley
1 oz/30 g	fresh cilantro (coriander)

12½ oz/350 g	onions
2 oz/50 g	garlic
½ tsp	ground cumin
¼ tsp	paprika powder
⅘ cup/150 g	golden raisins
	salt and pepper

For the garnish:

⅓ oz/10 g	flat-leaf parsley
1 oz/25 g	sesame seeds

Oxtail with garbanzo beans and raisins is a very popular dish in Morocco. Oxtail is much prized in Morocco, and it is also sometimes cooked in an onion sauce with raisins, or it may be cooked with vegetables for many couscous dishes. However, mutton tail is generally more commonly eaten in Morocco. Dried, it enriches a delicious couscous served at the Ashura festival.

Oxtail is considered a poor quality meat. To make it tender and aromatic, it needs to cook for a long time over a low heat in a highly flavored broth. In many countries, especially in France, the meat is cooked until it comes off the bone. The delicious pieces of meat cooked in this way are used for fillings, stews, or casseroles with ground beef, mashed potato, or similar ingredients. Here, the chef serves the oxtail still on the bone. Moroccan cooks are of the opinion that the taste and consistency of the meat is of the same order as that of the neck, which can be used to replace it in this recipe. Choose a large piece with plenty of meat on the bone

Garbanzo beans, cultivated in Morocco, are almost always dried before they are sold. When fresh, they have hardly any flavor of their own. In regional cuisine, they are found in couscous dishes, as an accompaniment to oxtail, in salads, and in dishes with shank of veal.

The raisins, allowed to swell in the sauce, give a touch of sweetness to the dish. They are produced in the wine-growing regions around Meknès, Fez, and Marrakesh, and are available on the market in golden, reddish, or almost black variations. Weddings, official occasions, and religious festivals are almost unthinkable without raisins and almonds.

Soak the garbanzo beans the evening before. In a large pan, heat both types of oil. Place the pieces of oxtail into the hot oil.

On a chopping board, chop the parsley, fresh cilantro, peeled onion, and garlic with a knife. Add to the meat. Fry for a few moments, on a high heat, stirring.

Season with salt and pepper, cumin and paprika. Stir for a few moments on the heat, to allow the spices to develop their full aroma.

with Raisins

Drain the garbanzo beans and add them to the pan with the meat.

Cover all ingredients with water. Cover the pan and simmer for at least 2 hours on a low heat, until the meat begins to loosen off the bones.

15 minutes before the end of the cooking time, add the raisins to the meat. Bring to the boil. Arrange the meat on plates with the garbanzo beans and raisins. Garnish with parsley and sesame seeds.

Breast of Guinea Fowl

Preparation time: 45 minutes
Cooking time: 55 minutes
Difficulty: ★

Serves 4

4	breast fillets of guinea fowl
1	onion
3 tbsp/45 ml	vegetable oil
1 tsp	ground cinnamon
½ envelope	yellow food coloring
1 tsp	ground ginger
¼ cup/50 g	sugar

1 tsp	saffron threads
	salt and white pepper

For the couscous filling:

1¼ cups/200 g	fine semolina
4 tbsp/60 ml	vegetable oil
¼ cup/50 g	sugar
³/₅ cup/100 g	raisins
²/₃ cup/100 g	blanched almonds
1 tsp	ground cinnamon
½ stick/50 g	butter
1 tsp	orange flower water
	salt

For Moroccans, cooking *seffa* is a strong part of their culinary heritage. *Seffa* consists of a sweetened couscous and is flavored with cinnamon and orange flower water. Although this is a specialty from Fez, it is now known well beyond the borders of the royal city. In most families, *seffa* is eaten as a dessert with a glass of milk. Based on this Middle Eastern sweet dish, Abdellah Achiai has created a filling for breast fillets of guinea fowl.

Guinea fowl originally came from Africa, where there are still a few wild varieties today. The Romans called them "Numidian" or "Carthaginian chickens." They are very aromatic and tasty. The chef recommends trying the recipe with pigeon or partridge.

Like all inhabitants of the Maghreb, Moroccans have a taste for semolina. To make semolina, durum wheat is first roughly cleaned and then moistened to allow the husk and

the germ to be removed more easily from the grain itself. This is then ground in several milling processes. Between each stage in the milling—from very coarse to fine—the small pieces of grain, the semolina, are sieved. Whether the couscous is a success or not depends on the quality of the grain, but also on the preparation by hand. It is essential to cook the couscous in several stages in the top part of a couscous steamer.

In North Africa, sugar is produced from date palms while cane sugar was produced in Asia thousands of years ago. Alexander the Great is alleged to have introduced the cultivation of sugar cane into the Mediterranean region in the 4th century BC.

Cut the little rolls of meat diagonally, as the chef has done, to display the couscous filling.

For the filling, salt the semolina and drizzle with the vegetable oil. With your hands, work in the vegetable oil and also a little water. Let the semolina swell a little and drizzle again with a little water.

Bring the water to the boil in the couscous steamer. Put the semolina in the strainer part on the top and steam for 15 minutes. Then place the semolina in a bowl. Once again, work in a little water. Once it has been absorbed, cook the semolina for another 15 minutes in the steamer.

Mix the semolina with the sugar, soaked raisins, almonds, cinnamon, butter, and orange flower water.

à la Achiai

Skin the breast fillets. Divide them lengthways and flatten them with the blade of a large kitchen knife. Spread the couscous filling along the whole length of the fillets.

Using your fingers, roll the fillets lengthways around the filling. Chop the onion.

Fry the fillets for 3 minutes in the oil. Add onion, cinnamon, food coloring, ginger, sugar, and saffron threads. Season with salt and pepper. Add 1 glass of water. Cook, covered, for 20 minutes. Reduce the sauce and strain. Cut the rolls of breast fillet diagonally. Arrange and serve.

Tride with

Preparation time:	*30 minutes*		1 envelope	Moroccan saffron powder for coloring
Cooking time:	*1 hour 25 minutes*		1 tsp	*ras el-hanout* (spice blend)
Difficulty:	★★		6 cups/1.5 l	chicken stock
				salt and pepper

Serves 4

For the tride pastry:

1	free range corn-fed chicken		4⅓ cups/500 g	flour
7 tbsp/100 ml	olive oil		1 pinch	salt
2	onions		1 tbsp/15 ml	oil
5	saffron threads			

Tride with a chicken is a feast. It is often served in the country at harvest festivals. It is also frequently offered to new mothers shortly after birth.

Tride pastry is similar to *yufka* pastry, but somewhat thicker and about the size of a crepe. The traditional style of making the dough is rather interesting. First of all, a dough is formed from flour, salt, oil, and water, then kneaded and shaped into a ball. It is then divided into several smaller balls. On a well-oiled work surface, the dough is teased out with the fingertips as thinly as possible. Charcoal is heated in a *brasero*, a kind of small barbecue, and a large, rounded pitcher is heated on it. As soon as this is very hot, the sheets of *tride* dough are slapped onto the walls of the pitcher until they are cooked. Some Moroccans make their task easier by preparing the *tride* sheets in a frying pan. This is the method the chef has chosen.

M'hamed Chahid recommends choosing a free-range, exclusively corn-fed chicken for this recipe. In Morocco, these chickens are known as *beldi*. Despite their grayish or yellowish skin and their not over-plentiful, very firm flesh, many Moroccans think they taste far better than factory-farmed chickens, although these may have paler and more succulent meat. Fry the chicken with the spices to make it deliciously golden-brown, cook the onions well and allow the flavors to penetrate deeply into the chicken. Only then should you pour on the chicken stock.

Don't forget to season the sauce with *ras el-hanout*. This complex spice mixture sometimes consists of up to a dozen different ingredients. Unfortunately, the use of this spice is today limited to recipes from the regional cuisine.

For the dough, place the flour in a bowl. Add salt, a glass of water, and oil. Knead the dough until you can form a ball. Divide the ball into several smaller balls.

Use your fingertips to stretch each small ball until thin, almost transparent discs are formed. Cook like crepes in a frying pan. Put aside.

Cut off both legs from the chicken. Do the same with the wings. Cut the carcass into four.

Chicken

Fry the chicken pieces in a pot in olive oil. Add the onions, cut into rings, saffron threads, saffron powder, salt, pepper, and ras el-hanout. Allow to fry for 10 minutes.

At the end of these 10 minutes, pour the chicken stock over the chicken pieces. Cover and cook for 1 hour.

Break up the trides by hand into large pieces and place them on a decorative serving platter. Place the chicken pieces on top and pour the sauce over everything.

Desserts & Pastries

Baghrir

Preparation time: 40 minutes
Resting time: 1 hour
Cooking time: 15 minutes
Difficulty: ★

Serves 4

1½ cups/250 g	dates from Tafilalet
⅔ cup/100 g	blanched almonds
1 tsp	ground cinnamon
1 tsp	orange flower water
2 tbsp	honey

For the baghrir batter:

2⅛ cups /250 g	flour
1½ cups/250 g	fine semolina
1 tsp	fresh yeast
3½ tbsp	baking powder
1	egg
	salt

For the garnish:

	honey
	crushed almonds

Baghrir are typical Moroccan crepes. The batter is made from flour, fine semolina, egg, raising agents, salt, and water, and they are eaten at any time of the day. They are frequently offered to guests as a sign of welcome and for this occasion they are drizzled with honey.

Traditionally, *baghrir* are made on terracotta tiles known as *zelij*. Moroccans insist that these delicious crepes are only perfect when they are full of a thousand little holes.

Abdellah Achiai combines this Middle Eastern sweet dish with the famous dates from Tafilalet. These dates, harvested in the splendid oases in the south of the country, come from a region with a name well known in the past. Here, where today a million date palms grow, the caravan road between Fez and Timbuktu once ran. For more than a thousand years, the capital of the region, Sijilmassa,

famous in Roman times, was a city to rival Fez and Marrakesh, and was one of the most important centers of Saharan trade. At one time, Jewish and Muslim merchants traded at the gateway to the Sahara in valuable fabrics, metals, dates, and salt.

These crepes filled with dates have a wonderful spicy taste. The cinnamon in them contributes its powerful, spicy flavor. The dried bark of the cinnamon tree, a spice essential in Moroccan cooking, can be recognized by its strong, penetrating scent.

To make orange flower water, the blossom of the orange tree is first soaked and then distilled. Orange flower water is not only used to add scent and flavor, but is also believed to have a calming effect.

For the baghrir, mix the flour and semolina. In another bowl, place yeast and baking powder, egg, salt and 1 glass of lukewarm water. Stir. Gradually work into the flour and semolina mixture. Mix well until a smooth batter is formed. Allow to rest for 1 hour.

On a cutting board, remove the stones from the dates and dice them into very small pieces.

Roast and crush the almonds, then put them in a bowl. Add the dates, ground cinnamon, and orange flower water.

with Dates

Mix the ingredients in the bowl and crush them further with a spoon. Add 2 tbsp of honey and mix again.

Put a ladleful of the baghrir batter into a non-stick frying pan and make crepes without adding fat.

Place the almond and date mixture onto the crepe and roll up or fold over. Drizzle with a little honey and garnish with crushed almonds.

Almond and

Preparation time: 20 minutes
Cooking time: 15 minutes
Difficulty: ★

Serves 4

7 cups/1 kg	almonds
²/₃ cup/150 g	sugar
4	eggs
1 pinch	ground cloves
3½ tbsp	baking powder
¼ tsp	vanilla extract
1 tsp	ground cinnamon
2¼ cups/250 g	powdered sugar

Fatima Mouzoun's crunchy, sugared cookies catch the eye of every gourmet. The whole almond placed in the middle of each cookie increases its attraction. Moroccans like to offer these tasty cookies to their friends with a glass of mint tea.

In Morocco, these cookies belong to a whole category of cookies and small pastries known as *ghriba*. There are two kinds: brown cookies such as these by Fatima Mouzoun, which are dusted with powdered sugar that is allowed to caramelize in the oven, and *m'soussa*, which are white. They are made with butter and are not spiced with cloves. The raising agents allow Fatima Mouzoun's cookies to rise when baking and at the same time give them the decorative little cracks in the surface.

Add only a small pinch of ground cloves to the dough as the powerful aroma, reminiscent of liquorice and violets, can quickly become dominant. If you use whole cloves, make sure you crush them very finely with a mortar and pestle. It is not very pleasant to bite on a piece of clove when trying one of the cookies!

Cloves are the stamens of the flower of the clove tree, which originated in the Moluccan Islands in Indonesia. The tree belongs to the myrrh family. To vary the aroma and flavor of the cookies, instead of cloves you can use grated nutmeg or mastic gum crushed with sugar.

This recipe also includes almonds, as do almost all the recipes for sweet foods in the region, used either whole or ground. In Morocco, there are many different kinds of almonds: very large or very tiny, sweet or very bitter. For these cookies, Fatima Mouzoun likes to use the little *louz beldi*, which look a bit rough but are very sweet.

Place the almonds, with their brown skins, onto a baking sheet. Roast for 5 minutes. Put 6½ cups/900 g of the almonds into a food processor and chop, keeping the others for the garnish.

Put the sugar into a bowl. Break the eggs onto it and add the ground cloves.

Add baking powder, vanilla extract, and cinnamon. Beat thoroughly with a whisk.

Clove Cookies

Add the roasted, chopped almonds to the mixture. Knead by hand to make a smooth dough.

Take a little dough in the hand and roll into little balls. Flatten these slightly.

Press one side of each ball into the powdered sugar. Press half a roasted almond into the center of each cookie. Place the cookies on an oiled baking sheet and bake for 10 minutes at 275 °F/140 °C.

Almond and

Preparation time: 30 minutes
Cooking time: 15 minutes
Difficulty: ★★

Serves 4

7 cups/1 kg	almonds
	oil for frying
1²/₃ cups/375 g	sugar
2 tsp	ground cinnamon

1 pinch	mastic gum
2 tbsp	butter
3½ tbsp/50 ml	orange flower water
2 or 3	eggs yolks
10 sheets	*yufka* pastry dough
2¼ lbs/1 kg	honey

On festive occasions, whole pyramids of *briouates* with almonds and honey are waiting to be devoured by the guests. Their crunchy golden-brown appearance means that they are almost irresistible. The crisp dough surrounds a soft filling of almonds, cinnamon, and orange flower water.

The most commonly found *briouates* resemble little triangular shoes with a spherical filling. The filling can, however, also be shaped into little sausages and then rolled in the dough like a cigar. They can then be deep-fried in oil and immediately afterwards carefully dipped in honey. If you find this method difficult, you can also make the filling into a long roll, roll it up in the dough and then cut it into shorter pieces. These are then brushed with egg yolk, sprinkled with chopped almonds, and baked in the oven.

Fatima Mouzoun recommends a simple method of cutting the *yufka* pastry dough into equal-sized pieces. Roll up the

sheet and cut it into pieces with a small knife. Next, unroll the strips and brush the upper surface with a little egg yolk. Then brush the rest of the pastry with oil. This makes the *briouates* hold together well when frying and the filling will not fall out.

As soon as the *briouates* have turned a nice golden-brown in the oil, take them out and put them in honey. This is the best way of absorbing the honey, and the surface will take on its special consistency due to the difference in temperature between the hot oil and the cold honey. The chef recommends a very aromatic thyme honey with a strong color. You can garnish the pastries by dipping the sides into chopped almonds, pistachios, or sesame seeds.

Put the almonds into a pot of boiling water and wait until the skin can be removed. Take out of the water with a slotted spatula, allow to cool slightly and squeeze them out of their skins.

Heat the oil in a frying pan. As soon as it is hot, add 1³/₄ cups/250 g blanched almonds and fry for 5 minutes. Chop in a food processor and put aside in a bowl.

Then add the remaining almonds to the food processor. Add the sugar and switch on the machine.

Honey Briouates

Place the almond and sugar mixture onto a plate. Add the fried, chopped almonds and mix. Make into a roll.

Add mastic gum, butter, orange flower water, and cinnamon to the mix and knead again until it forms a smooth mass. Then put the eggs in a bowl.

Cut the yufka pastry dough into strips. Place a small ball of filling onto one end of the strip. Fold over and over in triangle shapes until you reach the end of the strip. Brush with egg yolk. Briefly fry the briouates and then dip in the honey.

Fresh Fruit

Preparation time:	40 minutes
Soaking time:	5 minutes
Cooking time:	10 minutes
Difficulty:	★★

Serves 4

1	apple
1	kiwi
1	banana
1	pear
3½ oz/100 g	strawberries
1 cup/100 g	shelled walnuts

1	lemon
½ cup/100 g	sugar
2 tbsp	orange flower water
½ stick/50 g	butter
4 sheets	*yufka* pastry dough
1	egg yolk
	oil for frying

For the garnish:

⅜ cup/50 g	powdered sugar
⅔ oz/20 g	ground cinnamon

If you ever enjoy the privilege of being the guest of a Moroccan family, you will be able to taste *briouates*, little fried envelopes of pastry with almond paste. The chef wanted to modernize these traditional pastries and has therefore used a filling made from fresh fruit.

The ancient Romans prized strawberries, which they came across when occupying Morocco. According to legend, these berries, rich in vitamin C and minerals, give long life. Choose fresh, undamaged fruits, where the leaves at the stalk end are green and soft. Don't leave the strawberries lying in the water when washing them because they will turn soft. You can also make this recipe with other fruits of your choice, but avoid citrus fruit.

Each fruit is prepared separately. After chopping, pour over a mixture of water, lemon juice, sugar, and orange flower water and soak them briefly, then fry them in butter. This way the full aroma of the fruit, especially the banana is released. Bananas, originally from India, are today cultivated in all tropical regions. In general, bananas sold in the markets are still slightly green. They should therefore be allowed to ripen at room temperature. These nourishing fruits, a good source of energy, contain pectins that make them nice and creamy, and the small "apple bananas" available in Morocco contain refreshing malic acid. Bananas taste especially delicious combined with cinnamon.

Kiwi fruit, or Chinese gooseberries, can be recognized by their furry, brownish-green skins. When peeled, they reveal a brilliant green, juicy, aromatic, and slightly acidic flesh. When buying, choose firm kiwi fruit that can ripen at room temperature.

Peel apple, kiwi fruit, banana, and pear. Rinse the strawberries. Dice all fruit small and place each kind in an individual small bowl. Crush the walnuts.

Squeeze the lemon. Pour the lemon juice into a bowl. Add sugar and orange flower water. Pour a little of this mixture into each of the small bowls of fruit and allow to soak for 5 minutes.

Melt the butter in a pan. Fry, separately, the diced pear, apple, strawberries, kiwi, and banana.

Briouates

Drain the fruit and place in a bowl. Add the crushed nuts and mix.

Place the sheets of dough one on top of the other and fold first into halves, then into quarters. Cut into strips. Beat the egg yolk in a bowl and put aside.

Place the filling on the strips of pastry dough. Fold into triangles by folding them first to the right, then to the left. Stick down with egg yolk at the end of each triangle. Fry the briouates for 3–4 minutes. Lift out of the oil and sprinkle decoratively with powdered sugar and cinnamon.

Chabakia

Preparation time:	30 minutes
Resting time:	15 minutes
Cooking time:	10 minutes
Difficulty:	✵✵

Serves 6

5 oz/150 g	sesame seeds
1	egg
2 tbsp	white vinegar
1½ cups/200 g	almonds
1 tsp	ground cinnamon

1 tbsp	aniseed
½ stick/50 g	butter
7 tbsp/100 ml	olive oil
7 tbsp/100 ml	orange flower water
3½ tbsp	baking powder
1 pinch	saffron threads
1 pinch	mastic
4⅓ cups/500 g	flour
	oil for frying
2¼ lbs/1 kg	honey

During Ramadan, Moroccans generally break their fast after sunset with *harira* soup, served with dates and pastries, such as crisp *chabakia* with honey. In Fez, *chabakia* are known as *griwach*, and in central Morocco as *m'kharka*. These sweet ribbons are among the various pastries offered with coffee after a wedding feast. There is another kind of *chabakia*, made from orange-colored dough and rolled up into a turban shape. They are then dipped in syrup.

Normally, *chabakia* are made without almonds, and with sesame seeds as the foundation of the dough. Sesame seeds are called *janjlan* in Moroccan. For this recipe, some of the sesame seeds are ground and worked into the dough, while the rest are used for garnish. It is best to roast the sesame seeds without fat to allow them to develop their nutty aroma to the full.

Fatima Mouzoun flavors her dough with saffron threads, orange flower water, aniseed, and mastic, a resin from a type of acacia that grows in Egypt and the Sudan. In Morocco, it is available as pale yellow crystals, while in other countries it is usually available as a white powder. The chef crushes it in a mortar with a pinch of sugar. Also crush the saffron threads with a mortar and pestle.

The chef works the dough by kneading it repeatedly between the fingers and with the palm of the hand. During kneading, she makes the dough firmer by adding flour and chopped almonds. She tastes the mix from time to time, thus checking the quantity of water and orange flower water. The vinegar serves to keep the dough elastic.

Before serving, you could sprinkle the *chabakia* with sesame seeds, chopped pistachios, or almonds.

Dry-roast the sesame seeds in a frying pan. Put the egg, vinegar, blanched and chopped almonds, cinnamon, crushed aniseed, 3½ oz/100 g of the sesame seeds crushed in a food processor, melted butter, olive oil, and orange flower water into a bowl.

Beat the mixture with a whisk. Add baking powder, saffron threads, and mastic and then the flour. Knead firmly by hand until you have a firm, smooth dough. Roll into several large balls and allow to rest for 15 minutes.

On a floured work surface, roll the dough out thinly with a rolling pin. With a pastry cutter, cut the dough into a large rectangle, then into 6 smaller rectangles.

Taking one of the small rectangles, use the pastry cutter to make 6 parallel cuts, but not quite to the edges, Separate the strips with your fingers, press two of the corners together, and then the other two corners, allowing the strips in the middle to protrude.

Prepare the other chabakia in the same way. Put into hot oil and deep-fry until the chabakia are almost dark brown. Then scoop them out of the oil with a spatula.

Immediately place the chabakia into a deep plate with honey and turn in the honey with a spatula. Then drain them in a sieve. Sprinkle with the remaining sesame seeds.

Gazelle

Preparation time:	50 minutes
Resting time for the pastry:	15 minutes
Resting time for the gazelle horns:	8 minutes
Cooking time:	40 minutes
Difficulty:	★★

Serves 4

For the almond filling:

7 cups/1 kg	almonds
2¼ cups/500 g	sugar
2	egg yolks
1	unwaxed lemon

2 tbsp	butter
1 pinch	mastic
7 tbsp/100 ml	orange flower water
	oil for greasing

For the gazelle-horn pastry:

2⅛ cups/250 g	flour
1 tbsp	butter
1	egg white
7 tbsp/100 ml	orange flower water

For the garnish of the sesame seed horns:

4	egg whites
1⅛ lb/500 g	sesame seeds

Gazelle horns are veritable ornaments of Moroccan pastry making. They adorn many buffets set up for religious festivals. There they appear next to the essential *briouates* with almonds and honey, known as *m'hancha*, sesame seed horns and *chabakia*. Altogether, about 20–25 different kinds of delicate pastries will be on offer to the guests. The gazelle, a symbol of beauty, refinement, and elegance, has given its name to this pastry. In Morocco, it is known as *kaâba ghouzal*.

Fatima Mouzoun recommends making both gazelle horns and sesame seed horns based on the same almond mixture. The filling contains twice the quantity of almonds as sugar. If the almonds are chopped with the sugar in a food processor, it should be possible to form the mixture into little rolls by hand. If that won't work, do as the chef does: add a little orange flower water.

In traditional recipes, the filling contains ground cinnamon, which turns the mixture brown. For this reason, Fatima Mouzoun prefers to use lemon peel for aroma and flavor. Sometimes she also adds chopped peanuts to the almonds. When the filling is made into a little half-moon shape, it can simply be dipped into orange flower water and coated in powdered sugar—or wrapped in pastry and closed into a ring.

To make the pastry for the gazelle horns, the chef kneads the dough into a long, thick strand that she then presses firmly back together again, repeating this many times. Afterwards, she divides it into many balls, brushed with oil. This stops them from sticking together or drying out. Wrapped in film, they are left to rest for 15 minutes in the fridge.

For the gazelle-horn pastry, put the flour in a bowl. Add the melted butter and the egg white. Knead with water and add the orange flower water. Knead until a smooth dough is formed, similar to that used for tarts. Allow to cool for 15 minutes.

For the filling, scald the almonds and peel them. Put into a food processor with the sugar to chop.

Put the mixture onto a large plate. Add orange flower water and egg yolk. Grate the lemon peel over it, then add butter and mastic. Knead together well.

Horns

Oil a large plate. With oiled hands, roll the filling into little balls, then make "sausages."

For the sesame seed horns, first beat the egg whites lightly and then add half the almond mixture "sausages." Lay these briefly in the sesame seeds and then roll between your hands. Place on an oiled baking sheet and bake in the oven for 15 minutes.

For the gazelle horns, roll out a ball of pastry dough. Place the filling on the dough, fold it over and form a crescent shape. Prepare the other gazelle horns in the same way. Allow to rest for 8 minutes, then bake in the oven for 40 minutes.

Crepes with

Preparation time:	20 minutes
Proving time:	20 minutes
Cooking time:	3–4 minutes per crepe
Difficulty:	★

Serves 6

For the crepes:

3 cups/500 g	very fine semolina
½ tsp/2 g	salt

3½ tbsp	baking powder
1 cube	fresh yeast
2	eggs

For the sauce:

7 tbsp/100 g	butter
3½ oz/100 g	honey

Crepes with Atlas honey are eaten as a dessert and also for breakfast. These crepes, also known as *baghrir*, look rather like a honeycomb, due to the thousands of little holes in the surface. Moroccans like to offer *harira* soup with *baghrir* to women who have recently given birth.

For the batter, choose a very fine durum wheat semolina of deep golden-yellow color. This will give a good soft consistency to your crepes. Some cooks also mix a little flour with the semolina. Amina Khayar, however, prefers pure semolina to make a nice light dough. She mixes in baking powder and yeast in equal parts: she believes this gets the best results in creating small and evenly distributed holes in the crepes. The lukewarm water added also dissolves the raising agents and lets the batter rise better. Allow the batter to prove in a warm place to let it rise well.

Several regions in Morocco produce excellent honey. Atlas honey is viscous, the color of dark amber and has a well-developed flavor. Moroccans use it as an accompaniment to pastries and crepes or to spread on bread, and it tastes wonderful with a glass of tea with mint. Some meat dishes, such as shoulder of lamb with prunes and apricots or the lamb dish *m'rouzia*, also benefit from adding honey to the sauces.

The clarified butter needed for the sauce is easy to make. When the butter is melted, three layers form: an upper thin layer of foam, a thick yellow middle layer that is the pure butterfat, and a milky-white deposit. Skim off the white foam and then pour off the butterfat, leaving only the white deposit in the pan. Then stir the clarified butter into the honey and turn your crepes in the mixture.

Put the semolina into a bowl. Make a well in the center. Into the well, put the salt, baking powder, crumbled yeast, and the eggs.

Stir the mixture with a whisk. Gradually, while continuing to whisk, add lukewarm water.

Put the mixture into the bowl of a food processor. Mix until a smooth, pale yellow, creamy batter is formed. Pour into a bowl and allow to prove for 20 minutes in a warm place.

Atlas Honey

Heat a small, non-stick frying pan without fat. Pour in a small ladle of the batter. Fry the crepe on one side only until it is firm and looks like a pale gold honeycomb.

Melt the butter in a small pan. Allow to rest for a moment, then skim the foam off the top. Pour the pure butterfat through a fine sieve, leaving only the milky white deposit in the pan. Mix the clarified butter with the honey.

Directly before serving, dip each crepe briefly into the butter and honey mixture. Serve warm.

Fakkas

Preparation time: 20 minutes
Cooking time: 30 minutes
Difficulty: ★

Serves 4

1½ cups/200 g   almonds
1⅛ cups/250 g   sugar
8   eggs
1¾ sticks/200 g   butter
1 tbsp /15 ml   oil

1¼ cups/200 g   raisins
¼ tsp   vanilla extract
1 splash   orange flower water
3½ tbsp   baking powder
8⅔ cups/1 kg   flour

In Moroccan families, tea is served up to three times a day. It is traditional to offer a little bowl of *fakkas* with it, together with almonds, peanuts, dates, dried figs, and raisins. In the interior of the country, people make very small *fakkas* and serve them to guests at the New Year Festival, *Ashura*.

Like many Moroccan pastries, *fakkas* are distinguished by the generous quantity of almonds they contain. Almond trees, which belong to the rose family, bear fruit from June to the end of September. The almonds are harvested by being shaken or struck out of the tree, the gray-green fuzzy fruit flesh around the shell, which is inedible, is removed. The almonds are then dried. Dried almonds are available all the year round in many different forms: in their hard shells, as a kernel only with their brown skins, peeled, or even ready chopped.

The chef sometimes uses crushed aniseed, sesame seeds, or walnuts instead of almonds. If neither almonds nor walnuts are available, she kneads sesame seeds into the dough. The raisins, which make the dough sweet and juicy, are produced in the north-west of Morocco, in the region around Khmissat and T'ifelt. In the markets, you can buy reddish, golden, or dark raisins.

Fatima Mouzoun forms the dough into *fakkas* in the shape of little baguettes, baked golden-brown in the oven and then cut into thin slices, barely one-fifth of an inch thick. These slices must be cut to regular sizes if they are to look good. The chef recommends brushing the rolls of dough with egg yolk to produce an appetizing golden-brown color in the oven. As soon as they are cooked, they are allowed to harden overnight (they can also be put in the freezer). Then the long rolls can be cut diagonally into slices easily.

Crush the almonds in a mortar and pestle, but coarsely enough for some largish pieces to remain.

Place the sugar and 7 eggs in a bowl. Beat with a whisk until the mixture is pale yellow and foaming.

Add the softened butter, oil, crushed almonds, raisins, vanilla extract, and orange flower water. Beat lightly and place on a large plate.

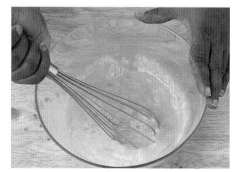

Work in the baking powder and the sieved flour with your hands. Continue to knead until you have a firm, smooth dough. Divide this into several balls.

Shape each ball into a roll, about 8 inches/20 cm long and 1 inch/3 cm thick. Brush with beaten egg yolk. Place the rolls on an oiled baking sheet and bake for 15 minutes in the oven until golden-brown. Allow the fakkas to cool.

Place the fakkas on a chopping board. Cut diagonally into slices about 1/5 inch/5 mm thick. Bake in the oven for another 15 minutes until the slices are golden-yellow.

Figs with

Preparation time: 15 minutes
Cooking time: 15 minutes
Difficulty: ✫

Serves 4

2¼ lbs/1 kg fresh figs
½ stick/50 g butter
3½ oz/100 g thyme honey
5 oz/150 g fresh goat's cheese

For the garnish (as desired):
    mint leaves

Although there are many lovely Moroccan desserts consisting of small pastries with dried fruit, there are no traditional sweet dishes with fresh fruit. Various kinds of fruit are offered in a basket or served in sweet salads with cinnamon and orange flower water. M'hamed Chahid has proved his creativity once again and proposes lightly frying quartered figs in butter, pouring a syrup of thyme honey over them and serving with goat's cheese.

M'hamed Chahid comes from Tangier: northern Morocco is equally famous for its figs and for its goat's cheese and honey. The chef uses thyme honey that is as dark as chocolate. If you can't get thyme honey, simply use ordinary honey and warm it in a pan with a sprig of thyme.

For this dessert, the chef likes to use white figs, which are ideal because of the combination of colors. However, purple-skinned figs are also suitable. Two kinds of figs are on offer in Moroccan markets. The *bakour*, which ripen in a single week, are the source of the proverb "The seven days of figs soon pass." All those who boast of their successes and forget that inevitably other times will follow get to hear this proverb. The other variety of fig is very sweet and has a much longer season.

Choose a good quality fresh goat's cheese. It is still made by hand in the Rif Mountains, with the milk churned by being shaken in a goatskin. The cheese is then allowed to drain for three or four days wrapped in a cloth. Little cubes of fresh goat's cheese taste wonderful with the fruit covered with honey syrup.

Rinse and wash the figs. Remove the stalks. Cut the fruits, starting from the top, into regular thirds or quarters.

Cut the butter into pieces. Melt in a pan until it foams.

Put the quartered figs into the hot butter. Shake the pan in order to coat the figs well with the butter, and brown them evenly.

Thyme Honey

Remove the figs and set aside. Instead of the figs, now add the honey to the melted butter. Stir with a wooden spatula. Reduce the sauce over a medium heat, stirring continuously.

Cut the goat's cheese into little cubes.

Pour the honey syrup onto a plate. Place the cubes of cheese in the middle, then arrange the figs in a ring around them. Garnish with leaves of mint.

Mohamed Tastift's

Preparation time: 25 minutes
Cooling time: 2 hours
Difficulty: ★

Serves 4

²/₃ cup/100 g   dates
6 tbsp/90 ml   milk
7 oz/200g   fresh goat's cheese
½ cup/100 g   sugar

3 tbsp   orange flower water
3 leaves   gelatin
½   lemon
1 tsp   vegetable oil

For the garnish:
   honey
   dates
   mint leaves (as desired)

This cheesecake has been created by Mohamed Tastift, who works in the "Berbére Palace" hotel in Ouarzazate and uses only regional products for its preparation. The recipe is based on fresh goat's cheese, dates, and honey.

Fresh goat's cheese, highly prized by the Berbers, is made exclusively from goat's milk. It contains less than 45 percent fat and is neither matured nor fermented. Fresh goat's cheese tastes very mild, sometimes a little acidic. Pastry chefs like to use it for desserts, but it does not keep for long. According to preference, you may replace it with ricotta, which has a more neutral taste.

This cheesecake goes perfectly with dates. There are more than three million date palms growing in Morocco, mainly in the south of the country, and the sweet fruits are given a place of honor in the culinary repertoire.

Dates are a symbol of hospitality in Morocco and for this reason, among others, they are an ingredient in many sophisticated recipes. When fresh, they have a pleasantly soft, creamy consistency.

Honey is highly valued by the people living in Ouarazazate. Color, taste, and consistency vary according to the type of flowers preferred by the bees. The most widespread varieties are clover, rapeseed, and lucerne honey. For this recipe the chef recommends acacia honey, distinguished by its mild sweetness.

This cheesecake by Mohamed Tastift is very simple to make, and is a delicious and sophisticated dessert that tastes delightful, even for breakfast.

Remove the pits from the dates and dice.

Warm the milk. In a food processor, mix the goat's cheese with sugar, orange flower water, and the lukewarm milk.

Prepare the gelatin according to the directions on the packet and add to the cheese mixture. Squeeze the half lemon and add the juice to the mixture as well. Mix once more in the food processor.

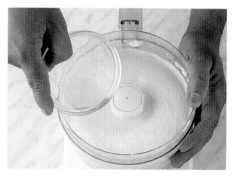

Cheesecake

Place the diced dates in a bowl and pour the cheese mixture over them. Stir.

Brush some little molds with oil. Spoon the mixture into these. Allow to set in the fridge for 2 hours.

Loosen the cheesecakes with the blade of a knife. Put onto plates and pour 1 tbsp of honey over each.
Garnish with dates and mint leaves.

Date Bites

Preparation time: 40 minutes
Resting time
  for dough: 15 minutes
Cooling time: 15 minutes
Cooking time: 25 minutes
Difficulty: ★

Serves 6–8

For the dough:
1¼ sticks/150 g butter
2 oz/50 g margarine
¼ tsp vanilla extract

2⅛ cups/250 g flour
8 eggs
1 pinch instant coffee

For the date filling:
11¾ cups/2 kg dates
1 pinch ground cinnamon
⅓ oz/10 g mastic
1 pinch grated nutmeg
7 tbsp/100 ml orange flower water

The guests of the "Beach Club" hotel in Agadir hold Abdelmalek al-Meraoui's date bites in high regard. The little rhomboid pieces are both simple and sophisticated: two thin layers of sweet dough surrounding a delicious date filling. In Morocco, such little pastries are very popular, and there are many recipes with dates. The date paste produced by the chef is also suitable for filling *yufka* dough "cigars," *rziza*, and *m'semmen* (crepes).

It is the mixture of butter and margarine that prevents the sweet dough from tearing when you make it. The chef mixes butter and margarine by hand and squeezes the shortening firmly through his fingers to eliminate even the smallest lump. If the dough becomes too soft, he adds a little flour and continues to work it. The finished dough is shaped into a ball and then needs to rest in the fridge. In this way, it keeps its shape.

The date filling makes the bites marvelously soft and sweet. Abdelmalek al-Meraoui generally uses *tmar* dates with very soft flesh. During Ramadan, Moroccans often eat these dates either fresh or dried. On festive occasions, they like to offer their guests milk and *tmar* dates as soon as they arrive.

Orange flower water serves to refine many desserts. It is most often made from the flowers of bitter orange trees. Sometimes bitter oranges are also puréed with the dates to make a filling.

To garnish the pastries, the chef takes a brush and coats them with a mixture of beaten egg and instant coffee (or caramel). With a fork, he then draws lines on the surface and this gives them an attractive golden-yellow pattern after baking.

Put the butter and the margarine into a bowl. Knead together well with your hands. Add vanilla extract, flour and 7 eggs. Beat all together well at first, then knead to make a good smooth dough. Roll into a ball and allow to rest for 15 minutes in the fridge.

For the filling, bring water to the boil in the lower part of a couscous steamer. Remove pits from the dates and place them in the strainer part of the couscous steamer. Cover and steam for 10 minutes, then skin the dates.

Place the dates in a bowl. Sprinkle with cinnamon, mastic, and nutmeg. Purée in a food processor. Add orange flower water and mix again.

à la al-Meraoui

Roll out the dough with a rolling pin. Cut a large rectangle, corresponding to the size of the baking pan, out of the dough. Roll the rest of the dough out again and cut another rectangle of the same size.

Line a rectangular baking pan with baking parchment. Cover with one rectangle of dough. Spread the date paste on top of it and smooth down with a spatula or the back of a spoon. Cover with the second rectangle of dough.

Beat 1 egg with a little instant coffee. Spread onto the dough with a brush. Place in the chill compartment for 15 minutes. Cut the cake into rhomboids. Place on a baking sheet and bake in the oven for 15 minutes at 430 °F/220 °C.

Ghriba with

Preparation time: 30 minutes
Cooking time: 10 minutes
Difficulty: ★

Serves 4

10½ cups/1.2 kg shelled walnuts
4 egg whites
1⅛ cup/250 g sugar
1 tbsp butter
1 tsp ground cinnamon
¼ tsp vanilla extract
  oil for greasing

Whenever there are celebrations in Morocco, *ghriba* are often among the 20 different kinds of cookies and pastries offered to guests. *Ghriba*, based on walnuts or almonds, are in fact offered only on special festive occasions or to guests of very high status.

For many Moroccans, almonds and walnuts are still very expensive. For this reason, they sometimes make *ghriba* from sesame or peanuts, or even just from flour. They then flavor them, according to taste, with aniseed, cinnamon, or crushed cloves.

Moroccan pastry chefs use almonds, sesame seeds, raisins, dates, and, less frequently, walnuts or pistachio nuts. In Morocco, excellent home-grown walnuts are available, though production is small, and nuts are additionally imported from Spain and France.

In this recipe, which is fairly easy to make, it is only the baking in the oven that requires some care. Keep a good eye on the cookies while they are in the oven, as the nuts on top of the *ghriba* brown very quickly. As a further precaution, brush the baking sheet with oil before baking: this will prevent the *ghriba* from burning from below, and make them easy to remove from the sheet after baking.

Fatima Mouzoun sometimes makes her *ghriba* round, on other occasions she forms them into "eye" shapes with tapered ends. For a buffet, she will wrap the ghriba in little individual paper frills: not only practical, but also decorative.

Roughly chop 8⅔ cups/1 kg shelled walnuts in a food processor. Keep the remaining nuts for the garnish.

Place the egg whites and the sugar in a bowl. Beat with a whisk until the mixture turns white.

Put the beaten egg white and sugar onto a large plate. Add the softened butter, ground cinnamon, vanilla extract, and chopped nuts. Knead by hand until a smooth dough is formed.

Walnuts

Take small portions of the dough into your hands and form little balls.

Garnish each ball with one of the walnut kernels put aside.

Place the ghriba on an oiled baking sheet. Bake in the oven for 10 minutes.

Haloua

Preparation time: 30 minutes
Cooking time: 20 minutes
Difficulty: ★

Serves 4

For the dough:
2²/₃ cups/300 g   flour
2¹/₄ sticks/250 g butter
4 tbsp   orange flower water

For the filling:
1¹/₂ cups/250 g   dates
²/₃ cup/100 g   almonds
                   oil for frying
¹/₂ cup/50 g   shelled walnuts
¹/₂ tsp   ground cinnamon
4 tbsp   orange flower water

For the garnish:
2¹/₄ cups/250 g   powdered sugar

The term *haloua* covers all kinds of sweet foods and pastries, and among them are the 20 or so different types of sweet cookies and pastries that are served on festive occasions. Here, Fatima Mouzoun introduces us to little pastries, shaped like small ships, that melt in the mouth. They are made from little circles of dough with a small amount of filling. The dough is folded over the filling and the ends pinched together with the fingers. Sometimes Fatima Mouzoun also shapes the dough into balls and decorates them with a fork. You can let your imagination run free and cut the *haloua* into all kinds of shapes.

There are many different varieties of date growing in the Moroccan palm groves. The chef recommends using only best quality dates: she prefers the large *majhoul* dates, which are rather dark but creamy, sweet, and juicy. If you wish, you can replace the dates with prunes or dried figs.

Almonds, known as *louz*, are an essential ingredient in all Moroccan cookies and pastries. Almond trees grow mainly in the south of the country, in the regions of Agadir and Rachidia—that is to say, in the Sous area.

For pastries, Fatima Mouzoun only uses almonds that have been stored with the brown skins on. Blanched almonds dry out very quickly, and if they are used for baking the result is often too firm and dry. To blanch almonds, put them into boiling water and wait until the skin begins to loosen. Then put them onto a work surface, take each one between two fingers and squeeze one end. The almonds will then slip out of their skins.

For the filling, put the dates onto a serving platter and remove the stones.

Put the almonds into a pot of boiling water. When the skins bubble, scoop out the almonds with a slotted spatula and then remove the skins.

Heat the oil in a pan. When it is very hot, put in the blanched almonds and fry for 5 minutes on a high heat until golden-brown. Take out of the oil with a slotted spatula and drain. Chop in a food processor and put aside in a bowl.

with Dates

Chop the dates and shelled walnuts in the food processor. Add chopped almonds, cinnamon, and orange flower water. Continue to use the food processor until a smooth paste is formed. Use your hands to make small "date" shapes out of the paste.

For the dough, put the flour onto a plate and make a well in the center. Put the softened pieces of butter into the well. Knead by hand. Work in the orange flower water. Knead well together and roll the dough into a ball.

Take a small ball of dough in your hand and squeeze flat. Place one of the "dates" on it and fold the dough over the top. Pinch the ends together. Form the other haloua in the same way. Bake for 15 minutes in the oven. Allow to cool and sprinkle with powdered sugar.

Vegetable

Preparation time: 15 minutes
Difficulty: ✶

Serves 4

Beet juice:
1⅛ lb/500 g	beets
1⅛ cups/250 g	sugar
2	oranges
1 tbsp	orange flower water
2 sprigs	fresh mint

Carrot juice:
1⅛ lb/500 g	carrots
1⅛ cups/250 g	sugar
2	oranges
1 tbsp	orange flower water
2 sprigs	fresh mint

Cucumber juice:
1⅛ lb/500 g	large cucumbers
1⅛ cups/250 g	sugar
2	oranges
1 tbsp	orange flower water
2 sprigs	fresh mint

Abdelmalek al-Meraoui has put together three vegetable juices as desserts that are not only good for your health but are refreshing and easy to digest. The chef flavors all the juices with the same ingredients, regardless of the type of vegetable used. He uses sugar, orange juice, mint, and orange flower water to give them that unmistakable Moroccan touch. Gourmets can also replace the sugar with vanilla sugar and the orange flower water with rose water.

As in many other countries, in Morocco, cucumbers are mainly served as a salad, finely sliced or grated and seasoned with salt, pepper, and olive oil. Sometimes cucumbers are sugared and served as a dessert. People in Morocco also like to mix them with yogurt and enjoy them as *raib*. Beets, by contrast, are eaten only in salads. Salt, pepper, olive oil, and cumin are used to emphasize their strong flavor.

For the carrot juice, use fairly young carrots. If the carrots are older and harder, when blending or juicing add a splash of orange juice. If you don't use a blender or juicer, strain the puréed carrots in order to keep back the fibers. Put the purée in a fine sieve over a bowl and push it through with the back of a spoon or a small ladle, in order to gain as much juice as possible. In order not to mix the vegetable juices, take the trouble to rinse the bowl after sieving each type of vegetable.

The orange juice should be pressed from navel oranges. These are cultivated on plantations in the neighborhood of Agadir. The area is known for its wonderful oranges. Other very good areas for orange growing are in the north-west of the country in the Sidi Kaseim and Berken area.

Peel the carrots, beets, and cucumbers. Cut the cucumbers and carrots into thick slices. Quarter the beets.

Process the pieces of carrot, cucumber, and beet separately in a blender or juicer. If necessary, strain afterwards.

Halve and squeeze all the oranges. Put the juice aside. Save some orange zest for the cucumber juice garnish.

Juice Trio

Add sugar and orange juice to the 3 vegetable juices.

Then add the orange flower water to the 3 vegetable juices.

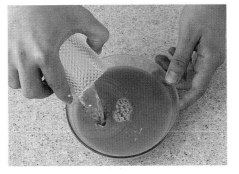

Chop the mint very finely and add to all 3 juices. Put the juice into attractive bowls. Garnish the cucumber juice with orange zest, the beet juice with mint leaves, and the carrot juice with finely chopped mint.

Madame Berdugo's

Preparation time: 50 minutes
Soaking time: 12 hours
Cooking time: 3 hours 10 minutes
Difficulty: ★★

Serves 4

For the eggplants:

2¼ lbs/1 kg	dwarf eggplants
1 tsp	baking soda
1 tsp	cloves
1 tsp	ground ginger
1 tsp	ground cinnamon
2¼ lbs/1 kg	sugar cubes
2 tbsp	honey
2	lemons

For the pomelos:

3⅓ lbs/1.5 kg	unwaxed white pomelos
3⅓ lbs/1.5 kg	sugar cubes
¼ tsp/1 g	alum
¼ tsp/1 g	mastic

For the oranges:

| 3⅓ lbs/1.5 kg | unwaxed navel oranges |
| 3⅓ lbs/1.5 kg | sugar cubes |

"For my daughter . . ." These words start off a letter from Madame Berdugo to her children, in which she sets down the recipe for her famous sweet treat, or rather, passes it on. Victoria Berdugo comes from Tangier and this recipe is reminiscent of *Pessach*, Passover, the Jewish spring festival celebrated with delicious sweet dishes. The preserved fruit is usually served to the guests in handsome crystal goblets.

All lovers of fruit confit will be won over by Madame Berdugo's nibbles. If stored in airtight closed Mason jars, the confit will keep for a long time. This old family recipe contains three different types of confit. The most original, undoubtedly, is the one with the eggplant. There are many different kinds of eggplant. Try to obtain very small, dark purple, elongated eggplants. Before cooking, prick them several times with a fork.

Oranges are also included in the sweet delicacies. This winter citrus fruit contains plenty of vitamins A and C and is well suited to preserving in this way. The chef recommends using navel oranges, because their thick, rough peel is easy to remove. Navel oranges are esteemed for their juicy, sweet flesh and have almost no pips.

Pomelos are the result of a cross between grapefruit and oranges made in America in the 19th century. Their thick white or pink peel is easy to remove. These hybrids contain very aromatic fruit flesh, even if it is a little less juicy than that of grapefruit.

These nourishing sweet treats created by Madame Berdugo are little miracles, displaying all the sophistication of Middle Eastern cuisine.

The evening before, thinly peel the zest off the pomelos with a vegetable peeler. Grate the oranges. Place the oranges and pomelos separately in large bowls of water and soak for at least 12 hours.

Remove the stalks from the eggplants. Prick the flesh with the tines of a fork. Place in cold water with 1 tsp baking soda for 5 minutes. Then rinse thoroughly.

For the eggplants: wrap crushed cloves, ginger, and cinnamon in a piece of gauze. Syrup for the oranges and pomelos: boil 6⅔ lbs/3 kg of sugar cubes with 12 cups/3 l water for 40 minutes. Divide the syrup into 2 halves. For the pomelos, wrap the alum in a piece of gauze.

Nibbles

For the polemos, quarter the pomelos and remove the peel. Soak the peel in water, then boil in water for 15 minutes. Pour on cold water and allow to drain. Cook, covered, with three-quarters of the syrup, the prepared bags of gauze, and the mastic, for 2¹/₂ hours.

For the oranges, cut into the orange peel using a knife, then place the oranges in water. Cook in the water for about 15 minutes. Put into ice water. Squeeze out the water. Cook the fruits in the second portion of the syrup, covered, for about 2 hours.

For the eggplant syrup, boil the sugar cubes with 4 cups/1 l water for 40 minutes. Add the eggplant and the gauze bag of spices. Cover and cook for 2¹/₄ hours. Add the honey and lemon juice. Cook for another 10 minutes. Arrange the nibbles on a serving platter.

Millefeuille with

Preparation time:	*35 minutes*
Cooking time:	*25 minutes*
Difficulty:	☆

Serves 4

4 leaves	gelatin
8 sheets	*yufka* pastry
	oil for frying
6 tbsp	honey
¼ glass	orange flower water
2	plums

2	peaches
1	apple (Golden Delicious)
22	large strawberries
2 slices	pineapple
2	kiwi fruit
2 cups/500 ml	milk
½ cup/100 g	sugar
2–3 sticks	cinnamon
2	egg whites
8	mint leaves
4	walnuts

Bouchaïb Kama has here created a very decorative and colorful dessert, with a tempting crisp consistency. Various small pieces of fruit have a syrup of honey and orange flower water poured over them and are then arranged on fried triangles of *yufka* pastry. This forms several alternating layers of fruit and fried pastry. To serve, the millefeuilles are topped with a small meringue, slices of strawberry, and mint leaves. Finally, a splash of strawberry sauce rounds off this sophisticated delicacy.

The peaches, plums, apples, strawberries, and kiwi fruit in this dessert all grow in Morocco. The Midelt region, to the west of the beautiful High Atlas, is famed for its peaches, plums, and apples. Golden Delicious, Mackintosh, and an elongated variety with a pale skin on one side and pinkish colored on the other are the apples mainly used for cooking in Morocco.

Strawberries are also cultivated on a large scale in Morocco. The big plantations are in the neighborhood of Asilah and Moulay Bousselham (between Rabat and Tangier), where the fields stretch to the horizon. The chef recommends using large fruit that can be easily sliced.

The fruits will stay on the sheets of pastry without difficulty, as the honey and gelatin stick them down. A great deal of honey is eaten in Morocco and there are many varieties. For this recipe, any blossom honey will do.

If you poach the beaten egg white, make sure the milk is not too hot, or the egg white will collapse. As soon as the meringues are cooked, drain them on kitchen paper. When stacking the millefeuilles, brush honey and gelatin over the triangles of pastry before placing the pieces of fruit onto them.

Soak the gelatin in cold water. Cut the yufka pastry into large triangles. Fry on a slotted spatula dipped in very hot oil until they are golden-brown. Drain on kitchen paper.

Put the honey, mixed with a little water, in a saucepan together with the orange flower water and the soaked gelatin. Beat with a whisk until a smooth syrup is formed.

Wash the plums, peaches, apples, and strawberries. Peel the apple, pineapple, and kiwi fruit. Slice all fruit thinly (reserve 10 strawberries). Put all fruit, except for the kiwi fruit, into a bowl and pour over the syrup. Allow to harden in the fridge.

Honeyed Fruits

Place a triangle of fried pastry onto a dessert plate. On it, place alternating layers of fruit and pastry.

Finish with a final piece of pastry. Form the other millefeuilles in the same manner. Keeping two for the garnish, purée the reserved strawberries and strain to make a sauce. Heat the milk with a pinch of sugar and the cinnamon sticks.

Beat the egg whites with the remaining sugar until stiff. Poach portions of the beaten egg white in hot milk. Garnish each millefeuille with a meringue of egg white, slices of strawberry, leaves of mint, and crushed nuts. Pour on a little strawberry sauce and serve.

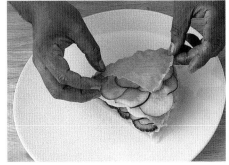

Pastilla

Preparation time: 30 minutes
Cooking time: 20 minutes
Difficulty: ✳

Serves 4

14 oz/400 g	*yufka* pastry
1	egg
	oil for frying

For the sauce:

1²/₃ cups/400 ml	milk

³/₈ cup/80 g	sugar
²/₃ oz/20 g	cinnamon sticks
3½ oz/100 g	cornstarch
2 tbsp	orange flower water

For the garnish:

2 oz/50 g	shelled pistachio nuts
²/₃ cup/100 g	blanched almonds
1 tsp/5 g	ground cinnamon
¼ cup/25 g	powdered sugar
1 tbsp	orange flower water
¹/₃ oz/10 g	fresh mint

The crispy triangles of pastry, first fried and then served with a cream flavored with orange flower water, are known in Morocco as *pastilla* with milk. To emphasize the sophisticated flavors better, the chef coats each of the triangles of pastry with an aromatic layer of crushed almonds and pistachio nuts.

It is rather difficult to prepare the dough for the *pastilla* yourself, although bought ready-to-cook sheets of pastry are never as fine and elastic as hand-made ones. Some women in Morocco have become very skilful in making *pastilla* dough and have specialized in it. They make the dough at home and sell it to shopkeepers. The thickness, appearance, firmness, and flavor of the pastry varies according to its origin. Fresh sheets of dough, known as *bastella* in Arabic, will keep in plastic wrap for only two or three days in the fridge.

In Morocco, pistachio nuts and almonds for the garnish are first roasted and then crushed with a wooden or metal pestle, the *mahraz*. You can also put them into a sealable freezer bag and break them up by hitting them carefully with a rolling pin or a meat mallet. This method prevents little pieces of almond or pistachio shooting off in all directions when they are chopped. To save time, you could also put the pistachio nuts and almonds into a food processor and chop them using the pulse button. Take care not to turn the nuts into powder.

Serve each portion of *pastilla* with some extra milk sauce in a bowl. This allows everyone to pour the sauce over the crisp pieces of pastry as desired.

Fold 1 sheet of pastry in half and cut down the middle. Fold each piece in half again to form a triangle. Stick down the edges of each triangle with beaten egg. Do the same with the other sheets of pastry.

Heat a little oil in a large frying pan. Brown the pastry triangles on both sides in the pan.

Pour the milk into a saucepan. Add the sugar and the cinnamon and bring the milk to the boil. Mix the cornstarch in a small bowl with a little hot milk and then add to the pot of milk, stir, and allow the milk to thicken over a low heat.

with Milk

Scent and flavor the resulting cream with orange flower water. Strain the cream and allow to cool.

Place the shelled pistachio nuts onto a baking sheet and roast in the oven. Crush with a pestle. Do the same with the almonds.

Mix crushed almonds, pistachio nuts, cinnamon, powdered sugar, and orange flower water. Pour a little cream onto each plate. Place the triangles of pastry on it and cover them with a layer of almonds and pistachio nuts. Garnish with mint leaves.

Fez-Style

Preparation time: 10 minutes
Cooking time: 15 minutes
Difficulty: ★

Serves 4

2½ cups/500 g   rice
4 cups/1 l   milk
⅔ oz/20 g   cinnamon sticks
½   unwaxed orange
½   unwaxed lemon

For the garnish:
1   orange
   mint leaves
⅔ oz/20 g   ground cinnamon

Rice pudding, Fez-style, is a delicious dessert, usually served in summer. It is most often eaten at the family table and is particularly popular with children, although of course not exclusively.

Many Moroccans see parallels between the culinary repertoire of Fez and the city itself. At table, the aromas of the Middle East unite in a mysterious way, before developing to the full. Outsiders need a little time to discover all the refinements of traditional cooking.

After wheat, rice is the most widely grown grain in the world. Rice grows in dry soil as well as in swampy areas or in heavily irrigated fields, and has been cultivated in China since 3000 BC.

When rice is cooked with cinnamon sticks, it takes on their full aroma as long as you do not use too much of this spice. Cinnamon is produced from the dried bark of the cinnamon tree and is famed for its mildly spicy flavor. Cinnamon sticks have a more intense flavor than ground cinnamon and their scent, too, is powerful and penetrating.

Abdellah Achiai also uses oranges to flavor and scent the rice pudding. He recommends choosing a slightly acidic variety. The round fruit with its orange-colored peel, sometimes veined in red, is rich in vitamin C and has orange or red fruit flesh. The best oranges are brilliant orange and quite heavy. They are not very delicate, so it is quite possible to store them for a few days at room temperature.

Put the rice into a bowl. Wash in cold water and drain.

Put the rice into a saucepan with 4 cups/1 l milk.

Add the cinnamon sticks to the pan with the milk and rice.

Rice Pudding

Slice the half orange thinly and add to the milk. Do the same with the half lemon. Cook the rice for about 15 minutes.

Remove the slices of orange, the half lemon and the cinnamon sticks. Put the rice into little bowls.

For the garnish, peel the orange, and cut into wedges, removing the dividing membrane. Arrange the wedges decoratively on top of the rice. Do the same with the mint leaves. Sprinkle with cinnamon.

Date Rolls

Preparation time: 40 minutes
Cooking time: 10 minutes
Difficulty: ★

Serves 4

3 cups/500 g	*majhoul* dates
1	lemon
½ cup/100 g	sugar
½ tsp/2 g	cloves
1 stick	cinnamon
1 tsp/5 g	ground cinnamon

1²/₃ cups/200 g	shelled walnuts
⅛ stick/10 g	butter
8 sheets	*yufka* pastry
1	egg yolk
4	navel oranges

For the garnish:

syrup (¼ cup/50 g sugar, cloves)
mint leaves

The chef uses only native products in the making of these date rolls on orange salad. In his opinion, this dessert is like his country. The *yufka* pastry, briefly baked, is reminiscent of the color of the desert sands; the dates pay homage to the oases; and finally, the oranges, cultivated mainly in northern and central Morocco, symbolize the fertility of this hospitable land.

This delicacy is easy to make and awards the dates a place of honor. There are 7,000 date palms growing in the palm groves of Tafilalet in the south. The *majhoul* dates harvested there are remarkable for their size and creamy soft consistency. They taste marvelous and are often combined with walnuts.

For this recipe, the walnuts need to be crushed with a pestle. Do not use a food processor. The blades turn so fast that the heat created then makes the nuts taste slightly oily.

Cloves are an important ingredient in the *ras el-hanout* spice mixture. To produce cloves, the blossoms of the clove tree are gathered before they open and then dried. In this dish, the cloves are allowed to develop their full, flowery aroma.

Moroccan oranges are highly regarded in many countries. They have an outstanding flavor and contain a lot of vitamin C. The oranges are sweeter or more acidic according to variety, and more or less aromatic in their flavor. For the orange salad, the chef uses navel oranges. Choose brightly colored, heavy fruit.

Remove the pits from the dates and dice the flesh finely. Squeeze the lemon and put the juice aside.

Cook the dates for about 5 minutes with ³/₈ cup/80 g sugar, the cloves, the cinnamon stick and the ground cinnamon. Add the lemon juice.

Crush the shelled walnuts with a mortar and pestle and add to the date mixture. For the garnish, prepare a white syrup: boil the sugar with the cloves in 2 cups/500 ml of water.

on Orange Salad

Melt the butter. Place 2 sheets of yufka pastry dough one on top of the other and brush with melted butter. Place the date filling on these and roll up the dough to form a "cigar."

Stick down the ends of the "cigar" with egg yolk. Brush once more with melted butter and sprinkle with the remaining sugar. Make the other 3 date rolls in the same way. Bake in the oven for 2–4 minutes at 350 °F/180 °C.

Peel the oranges and cut into small pieces. Arrange on a plate with the diagonally cut date rolls and drizzle with clove syrup. Garnish with mint leaves.

Sfouf

Preparation time: 30 minutes
Cooking time: 20 minutes
Difficulty: ☆

Serves 6

4⅓ cups/500 g   flour
3½ cups/500 g   almonds
                oil for frying
3⅓ lbs/1.5 kg   sesame seeds
2 tbsp   ground cinnamon

1 pinch   nutmeg
1 pinch   mastic
2¼ sticks/250 g butter
1 pinch   green aniseed
1⅛ lb/500 g   honey
7 tbsp/100 ml   orange flower water

Sfouf is eaten frequently in Morocco and is known by several different names: it is also called *selou* or *zameta*. Culinary customs connected with birth are of particular importance in Morocco, and new mothers are therefore often given a plate of *sfouf* to strengthen them.

Usually, *sfouf* has no honey in it and the sesame seeds are worked directly into the mixture. Fatima Mouzoun, however, shapes the *sfouf* mixture into a dome on a plate and dusts it with powdered sugar. She then decorates the dome with fried almonds. The chef has been inspired to create another form of presentation—she has spread the paste on a bed of roasted sesame seeds and sprinkled the top with a layer of more sesame seeds. The mixture is then cut into little squares and allowed to harden.

In this recipe, the *sfouf* is not baked. It is therefore necessary to brown the flour in the oven, to fry the

almonds, and to roast the sesame seeds. Dry-roasting without adding fat or oil imparts an additional nutty flavor to the sesame seeds.

Orange flower water and mastic gum also add their own particular touches. Moroccans prefer hand-made orange flower water, distilled in a container that looks rather like a couscous steamer. At weddings, the guests are sprinkled with orange flower water, and it is offered to the bridal couple to drink, together with milk, sugar, and dates.

Mastic gum is available in Morocco as yellowish crystals, which are crushed with a mortar and pestle together with a little powdered sugar. It comes from two types of acacias that grow in Egypt and in the Sudan.

Put the flour onto a baking tray and brown in the oven for 10 minutes. Then sieve it onto a large plate.

Peel the almonds and then fry them for 5 minutes in a frying pan with the oil. Allow to drain. In another pan, dry-roast the sesame seeds without adding fat, for 5 minutes.

Put 1⅛ lb/500 g roasted sesame seeds into the food processor and put the rest aside. Add the fried almonds and chop.

Put the sesame seed and almond mixture on the plate with the browned flour. Add the cinnamon, nutmeg, mastic, melted butter, crushed aniseed, honey, and orange flower water. Knead well to make a good smooth mixture.

Distribute 1¹⁄₈ lb/500 g roasted sesame seeds evenly over the bottom of a baking pan. Cover with the mixture you have just made. Sprinkle the remaining sesame seeds on top.

Press the sfouf down flat with the palm of your hand, then cut it lengthways and across to make regular squares. Leave until the sfouf has hardened.

Dried Fruit Tarte

Preparation time: 50 minutes
Soaking time: 15 minutes
Cooling time: 15 minutes
Cooking time: 20 minutes
Difficulty: ★★

Serves 4

For the pastry:

¾ stick/80 g	butter
1⅔ cups/200 g	flour
2	egg yolks
1 pinch	salt
¼ cup/50 g	sugar
2 tbsp/30 ml	rose water
1 tbsp/15 g	butter for greasing

For the cream:

4	eggs
½ cup/100 g	sugar
1 tsp	ground cinnamon
2 tbsp/30 ml	cream
2 tbsp/30 ml	rose water

For the filling:

½ cup/100 g	sugar
4 oz/120 g	dried figs
⅔ cup/100 g	dates
⅔ cup/100 g each	prunes, raisins
½ cup/80 g	preserved apricots
2 tbsp	rose water
1 tsp	sugar
3 tbsp	clear tart glaze

This dried fruit tart is the chef's own creation. It consists exclusively of products on offer in the Ouarzazate and Zagora regions. This very rich dessert is a temptation both for children and for adults.

To make this dish, you have to prepare a very firm, plain pastry. This pastry, usually reserved for especially fine baking, is then covered with dried fruit. Reserve part of the fruit and use it for decoration.

The apricots cultivated in Morocco are famed not only for their delicious flavor, but also because they contain many vitamins, especially vitamin A. These round, yellow to orange colored fruits with their fuzzy skins owe their name to the Catalan word *abercoc*. This in turn is based on the Latin *praecox*, meaning "early, premature."

The figs that Mohamed Tastift uses for this pastry are widely distributed all over the Mediterranean region. These fruits, originating in the Middle East, are eaten fresh or dried. They are very nourishing, rich in many vitamins, minerals and sugar, and mostly come from Turkey. They are dried in the sun, washed in seawater, and then sometimes treated with sulfur. They are eaten either on their own or filled with almonds or walnuts.

Just like the chef, most of the people living in Ouarzazate like rose water. The flavor goes wonderfully well with Mohamed Tastift's pastry. Every year, in the village of el-Kelaa, the capital of damask roses, 4,000 tons of buds of the little flowers are gathered. Rose water, especially widespread in Turkish cuisine, is also often offered to guests as a refreshment before the meal.

First make a syrup: bring 1 cup/250 ml of water to the boil with the sugar. Take the pot off the heat and add the dried figs. Soak for 15 minutes.

To prepare the filling, remove the pits from the dates. Dice small, and do the same to the prunes, apricots, and figs. Mix the rose water with the sugar. Soak the chopped fruit and the raisins in this mixture.

For the pastry, dice the butter into small cubes. Put the flour onto the work surface, add the cubes of butter, and rub between your hands. Add the egg yolks, 1 pinch of salt, sugar, and rose water. Shape the dough into a ball. Roll in plastic wrap. Put into the fridge for 15 minutes.

Ouarzazia

For the cream, beat eggs and sugar with a whisk. Add and beat in the ground cinnamon, cream, and rose water.

Grease a springform pan with butter. Roll out the pastry with a rolling pin, and then lay it in the springform pan. Press the pastry into the join of base and side of the tin with your fingers. Cut off any excess pastry around the top.

Place the soaked fruit onto the base of the tart. Pour on the cream. Bake in the oven at 350 °F/180 °C for 20 minutes. Mix the glaze with a little water, and brush over the tart.

The Chefs

Abdellah Achiai

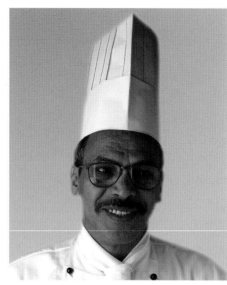

Mohammed Aïtali

Lahoussine Bel Moufid

Khadija Bensdira

Victoria Berdugo

M'hamed Chahid

Abdelmalek al-Meraoui

Bouchaïb Kama

Amina Khayar

Fatima Mouzoun

Mohamed Tastift

Abbreviations:

1 oz = 1 ounce = 28 grams
1 lb = 1 pound = 16 ounces
1 cup = 8 ounces *(see below)
1 cup = 8 fluid ounces = 250 ml (liquids)
2 cups = 1 pint (liquids)
1 glass = 4–6 fluid ounces = 125–150 ml (liquids)
1 tbsp = 1 level tablespoon = 15–20 g *(see below) = 15 ml (liquids)
1 tsp = 1 level teaspoon = 3–5 g *(see below) = 5 ml (liquids)

1 kg = 1 kilogram = 1000 grams
1 g = 1 gram = $^1/_{1000}$ kilogram
1 l = 1 liter = 1000 milliliters = approx. 34 fluid ounces
1 ml = 1 milliliter = $^1/_{1000}$ liter

*The weight of dry ingredients varies significantly depending on the density
factor, e.g. 1 cup flour weighs less than 1 cup butter.
Quantities in ingredients have been rounded up or down for convenience,
where appropriate. Metric conversions may therefore not correspond exactly.
It is important to use either American or metric measurements within a recipe.

© for the original edition: Fabien Bellahsen and Daniel Rouche

Design and production: Fabien Bellahsen, Daniel Rouche
Photographs and technical direction: Didier Bizos
Photographic assistant: Gersende Petit-Jouvet
Editors: Élodie Bonnet, Nathalie Talhouas
Assistant Editor: Fabienne Ripon
Coordination: Lahoussine Bel Moufid

Thanks to:
Moroccan Ministry of Tourism
Department of Promotional Planning and Coordination
National Moroccan Tourist Office
Chamber of Commerce of Oulja – Salé

Original title: *Délices du Maroc*
ISBN of the original edition: 2-84308-358-3
ISBN of the German edition: 3-8331-2437-7

© 2006 for the English edition:
Tandem Verlag GmbH
KÖNEMANN is a trademark and an imprint of Tandem Verlag GmbH

Translation from German: Susan James for Cambridge Publishing Management Limited
Edited by Laila Friese for Cambridge Publishing Management Limited
Proofread by Jo Osborn for Cambridge Publishing Management Limited
Typeset and managed by Cambridge Publishing Management Limited

Project Coordinator: Isabel Weiler

Printed in Germany

ISBN 3-8331-2033-9

10 9 8 7 6 5 4 3 2 1
X IX VIII VII VI V IV III II I